JINNAH'S

ISLAMIC VISION OF PAKISTAN

ANIS AHMAD

THE ISLAMIC FOUNDATION

Jinnah's Islamic Vision of Pakistan

First Published in 2025 by
The Islamic Foundation

Distributed by
Kube Publishing Ltd
MCC, Ratby Lane, Markfield
Leicestershire, LE67 9SY
Tel +44 (0)1530 249230
E-mail: info@kubepublishing.com
Website: www.kubepublishing.com

Author: Anis Ahmad
Cover design & typesetting: Nasir Cadir
Stock image: Shutterstock

A Cataloguing-in-Publication Data record for
this book is available from the British Library

ISBN 978-1-83592-016-9
eISBN 978-1-83592-017-6

Printed in Poland

"All sovereignty to govern belongs to Allah, He has commanded that you serve none but Him. This is the Right din (way), though most people are altogether unaware".

Yusuf 12:40

"...And consult them (wa shāwirhum) in the matters, and when you are resolved, put your trust in Allah".

al-'Imran 3:159

"Allah commands you to deliver trusts to those worthy of them, and when you judge between people, judge with justice".

al-Nisa 4:58

"(They are) those who, if we establish them in the land, establish (the system of) salah and give zakah, enjoin the right (ma'ruf) and forbid wrong (munkar).

al-Hajj 22:41

Contents

Acknowledgements

The present research is an outcome of a series of invited talks I delivered at the National Defense University, National University of Science and Technology and Riphah International University Islamabad. I appreciate their invitation and thank A.V.M. Faheem Ullah Malik (SI), former deputy President of N.D.U. who suggested the discourse to be developed into a monograph. I am indebted to Prof. Khurshid Ahmad for his continuous encouragement and his desire to get this research published.

I recognise the tireless help provided to me in typing and re-typing the manuscript by my executive assistant Mr. Mushtaq Ahmad and the assistance of Mr. Naufal of I.P.S. in its production. I am thankful to Mr. Shahid Awan for his personal interest in the publication of the book.

I dedicate this humble work to my parents, my wife Anisa, and my children Sumayyah, Yasir, Usamah and Nida who have always encouraged me in my academic pursuits.

This monograph is addressed to our coming generations who have been systematically kept in dark about the actual vision of the Quaid. It has been a gross intellectual dishonesty of the so-called liberals to hide the real vision of the Quaid from the nation under the pretext that he was secular and wanted a secular Pakistan. I have tried to let the Quaid speak for himself.

I hope our youth and my grandchildren Mu'minah, Muslim, Yahya, Aliyah, Aminah, Anas, Hana, Nuha, Umar, Ammar, Hamza, 'Afia and Khadijah when they are able to read and understand the dream of the Quaid, they and their generation will do their best to build our and their Pakistan as the Quaid wanted it to be. They must remember and thank Allah ﷻ for giving us a leader like the Founding Father Muhammad Ali Jinnah, who sacrificed his life along with unknown millions of Muslims in order to create Pakistan as an Islamic state.

Prof. Anis Ahmad Ph.D.
23, March, 2025

Preface

Objectivity in historical research is at least difficult, if not impossible. Historians and biographers often look into their subject matter with an unavoidable bias. When I was trained as a student of history and methodology of research in comparative religion and ethics, my own frame of reference were models developed mostly by European anthropologists, sociologists, psychologists and historians of culture and religion. The so-called quantitative methodology of data collection, classification and analysis was fascinating. Similarly, qualitative research was no less absorbing.

But after a sufficient period of involvement in academic research and familiarity with research methodologies and techniques, I started discovering the limitations of research and the impact of presuppositions on it. I noticed how basic assumptions influence social science research and impact apparently scientific conclusions we draw. A social scientist who is brought up in an empirical paradigm of knowledge where sense experience and physical verification is considered fact normally gives less importance to metaphysical, ethical and *ideological* dimensions.

Unfortunately, not all Muslim social scientists, including me, who are trained in an empirical research paradigm, realise their own research limitations. They look into their subject matter with a pre-conditioned mind and see "facts" as they are supposed to be seen. The half-full glass of water always appears to them half-empty.

Having said that, once we realise this limitation of scientific research, we start opening up and gradually realise our shortcomings and the need of objectivity in social science research. The idealists, functionalists, existentialists, post-modernists or the so-called liberals and enlightened approach issues from an already preconditioned mindset, consequently expected results are more or less predictable. Usually, we see facts with selected spectacles. This subjectivity is often never felt. Does it mean objectivity is a deception? Not exactly, as on the other hand I believe the realisation of the limitations of research and personal finitude helps us a lot in the development of a healthy and fair approach in research, though it may not be hundred percent objective.

Great personalities are generally studied using one or the other established research methodology within an epistemic paradigm. The century old concept of "hero worship" influenced historical writing in the academic world. Efforts were made to search for charismatic aspects in personalities under study. In the subcontinent, Shibli Nu'mani was no exception to it; perhaps influenced by Carlyle, he tried to identify heroes in Muslim history. Hali's book on life of Sir Syed (Hayat-e-Javed) was a continuation of this approach in writing history.

The study of the personality, ideas and convictions of the Quaid have been often studied with an already preconceived image of his personality as 'westernised', 'secular', nationalist and even 'communalist'.

The Western oriented scholars and media invariably have projected him as a secular person. The irony is that liberal writers have not only violated their own so-called objectivity, but not much intellectual honesty is observed either. They have disregarded dozens of *statements* of the Quaid which conflict with their self-perceptions of the Quaid. As intellectuals, they have every right to hold their own views on Pakistan's ideology and differ with the views of the Quaid. But it is totally intellectually dishonest to misrepresent the Quaid's personality. These so-called liberal intellectuals focus on only one speech of the Quaid, of 11 August 1947 in which he never said what they repeatedly attribute to him. They keep on putting their interpretation of the Quaid's Presidential address to the Constituent Assembly of Pakistan in the mouth of the Quaid with glaring dishonesty, until their interpretation assumes the status of an accepted fact. A recent study conducted by Salina Karim has documented that there is no recording file of that speech with All India Radio, which has been the only source of the speech, later on transcribed. This makes its historical validity seriously dubious. We know that the Quaid always read his written *statements* and speeches. But we have no original draft of this speech; all other speeches are fully supported by written record.

Even people like Justice Munir, who is supposed to be a responsible and fair person, disappoints us with his violations of basic research ethics by attributing a totally untrue statement to the Quaid. Saleena Karim's research work, *Secular Jinnah: What the Nation Doesn't Know*, exposes the intellectual dishonesty of the honourable Justice, which raises questions about the integrity of the person who enjoyed a high legal position.

The monograph that follows is a humble effort to ask the Quaid directly his views on Pakistan's ideology, instead of assuming and attributing to him one's own views. I let the Quaid speak for himself through his documented *statements* and let the readers decide about his *ideological* perspective.

The Quaid himself summarised his ideology for us in only three simple words: Faith (*Iman*), Unity (*Ittihad*) and Discipline (*Tanzim*). He gives top priority to faith (*Iman*), then to brotherhood (*Ukhuwah*), *Ittihad* of hearts, minds and aspiration; and last but not least refers to solidarity, (*Ijtima'yat*), order and discipline, or *Tanzim*. It appears that while referring to these three foundational principles, in the back of his mind he had the Qur'anic norms of *Iman, amanah, ukhuwah, ijima'iyah, sidq* and *mas'uliyyah*. These three words provide a solid basis for the development of education, scientific advancement, *halal* economy and building an ethically responsible society.

The Emergence of the Concept of *Millat*: An *Ideological* Community

The consequences of participation in the war for liberation of 1857 for the Muslims were catastrophic. The British tried to punish Muslims ruthlessly on account of their involvement in the so-called mutiny. Doors of employment were closed on them. The Muslim *qadis* lost their jobs. The Muslim education system was ruined. The Muslim intellectuals, in general, became defensive, apologetic, and in order to survive, they tried to prove their loyalty to the British. Sir Syed Ahmad Khan was among those who tried to prove the "loyalty of Muhammadans of India" to the crown. The unfriendly attitude of the British made the Muslims withdrawn and insecure. The Hindu leadership made use of this situation to their advantage and developed very cordial relations with the British. British colonialists treated the Muslims as an unfriendly religious minority. This view was further strengthened by the Hindu leadership who referred to Muslims as originally Hindus who converted to Islam. Therefore, as natives of the Indian subcontinent, they were essentially Indians. They totally ignored and disregarded the historical reality that for over eight centuries the Muslims ruled over India; consequently two parallel cultures, civilisations and distinct worldviews lived as neighbours for centuries.

The British, to marginalise Muslims and due to their own understanding of the nation state, concurred with the Congress that all who live in India were one nation. A serious gap of communication existed between the British and the Muslims. To build better communication with their subjects and in order to avoid clashes between the rulers and the ruled, after consolidation of their political power, the British introduced the Local Self Act in 1882.

Under this Act Municipal Councils, districts and constituencies were created on the basis of joint representation. This confirmed the Muslims' apprehensions that even in provinces and zones where Muslims were in majority, it was no longer possible for a Muslim candidate to succeed.

Sir Syed Ahmad Khan realised this problem and voiced Muslim concerns in 1882 and opposed the joint election of the representatives. It was no more a secret that, by introducing a British parliamentary system, the colonisers wanted to marginalise the role of Muslims and win the support of the Hindu majority in order to use them for their own purposes.

The British type of democracy was suitable for countries where there was no substantial difference of faith, language and ethnicity. Europe was essentially Christian and white and each state had its own territory and national language. The subcontinent, on the contrary, had no common faith, language or common history and culture. The heroes of Muslims were considered intruders by the Hindus. The Hindus themselves were divided in four major castes or classes. However, they were united against the Muslims, and aligned themselves fully with British colonialists. Demographically, Muslims during their rule of around eight centuries remained a minority. In this new situation, under the British parliamentary system, Hindus were to enjoy total majority in the provinces as well as in the centre. Muslims had no chance to gain strength in the parliament.

In this backdrop, the British took the initiative to establish the Indian National Congress in 1885 under the chairmanship of Mr. Hume, a senior British civil servant under the patronage of the British Viceroy, Lord Difren. The objective was to patronise the Congress in order to fully secure British interests with their full support. Until 1905, Congress took no interest in national issues and remained a puppet in the hands of the British. However, it tried to create unity among followers of various versions of who earlier could not think beyond their caste and creed. Since Congress had an alliance with the British, it had a major share in the civil service and became the main functionary of the British rule. In 1887, just two years after the founding of Congress, natives were allowed to officially enter the civil service; the ultimate beneficiaries were Hindus who had a major share in senior civil service positions.

The Indian Congress, though expected to represent local populations, worked only for the interest of Hindus. Sir Syed Ahmad noticed this exclusion of Muslims from all national affairs.

In the local body elections, a further condition was introduced that only those candidates who owned a property worth five thousand rupees could vote. Consequently, even in a place like Aligarh where Muslims were in the majority, no Muslim candidate could succeed. Sir Syed was compelled to publicly oppose the joint electorate and called Muslims to boycott the election in his address in Lucknow and Merath (March 1887).

In 1892, the British allowed more indigenous participation in central and provincial councils. Nevertheless, as expected in 1893 elections, Muslim candidates faced the same fate. Sir Syed proposed that in the Viceroy Council, membership of Muslims should get equal representation and these representatives should be elected by Muslims only. This was later called a separate electorate.

Due to the polytheistic trends in Hinduism, Muslim shrines were also visited frequently by Hindus. This gave a false impression that perhaps they were friendly toward Muslims. The elections fully exposed the alliance of the British and Indian Congress against Muslims. Yet, the traditional *Ullama* particularly from Deoband continued their full support to Congress on the one nation theory, and worked closely with the Indian Congress. They had no conflict with the Indian Congress because they neither contested in elections nor competed for civil service jobs.

Under the patronage of the British, the Indian Congress moved to have Hindi as the official language in place of Urdu. Fort William College, Calcutta, since 1804, was already the intellectual leader in this movement and had proposed writing *shudh* Hindi or Sanskritised Hindi in the *dewnagri* script instead of using Urdu script. Antony Mcdonald, a British Collector, when he became UP's Lieutenant Governor, officially declared Sanskritised Hindi in *dewnagri* script as the official language on 8 April 1900. This replaced Urdu as the official language in a province which was a major centre of Urdu.

Sir Syed passed away in 1898; Nawab Muhsin ul Mulk, the secretary of the Anglo Mohammadan Oriental College tried to protest, but the governor threatened him with the withdrawal of the grant for the College.

Hindus were further encouraged and introduced new festivals such as Ganpati puja, Gao puja and often played loud music in front of *masajid* at the time of prayers. They also established the militant wing of the Congress in 1905, like a paramilitary group fully trained in martial arts which later assumed the name Rashtriya Swayamsevak Sangh.

Nawab Muhsin ul Mulk took the initiative and approached all influential Muslims and a delegation consisting of 35 leaders under the leadership of Sir Muhammad Agha Khan met the Viceroy Lord Minto at Shimla on 1 October 1906 and briefed him on the discrimination and injustice faced by the Muslims. He agreed to the formation of a separate representative body of the Muslims and also later endorsed the idea of separate elections in his 1909 Minto Marley scheme.

Sir *Salimullah* Khan, Nawab of Dhakka, in the meantime, called a meeting of Muslim leaders from all over the India on 30 December 1906. Under the chairmanship of Nawab Waqar ul Mulk, a consultation was held. Nawab Waqar ul Mulk pointed out that in terms of population, Muslims are one fifth as compared to the Hindus, so when the British leave India those who are four times larger than Muslims are bound to rule the country. We can imagine what will happen to our *din*, honour, dignity, property and culture. We will have no choice but to be ruled by them. It is time to organise ourselves and have a representative body. This led to the creation of All India

Muslim League. Its first formal session was held on 29 December 1907 at Karachi. Muslims for the first time emerged as a separate people. Though the three main objectives of the League were: to be loyal to the British; the protection of Muslim political interests; and to try to reduce hatred of Muslims in other organisations. The founding of the Muslim League was the first step towards the protection of the Muslim identity and political interests.

Later events proved that the British and Hindu Congress worked with mutual trust and confidence against the interests of Muslims. In 1905, Bengal was divided in two administrative units. East Bengal had a Muslim majority while West Bengal had a Hindu majority. The bureaucracy had a Hindu majority and they did not like it. A violent movement was started by the Hindus of West Bengal. The British Rulers surrendered and, in 1911, the partition was withdrawn. This pleased the West Bengali Hindus and added to the frustration of Muslims. In the meantime, in order to widen a road, part of a masjid in Kanpur was demolished; Muslims held a protest on 13 August 1913 at Kanpur. The British and Hindu police treated the protesters with cruelty. Many Muslims were martyred and hundreds were injured.

In this hostile situation, the Lucknow Pact of 1916 was a landmark achievement which strengthened movement for Pakistan. It recognised separate elections and allowed a slightly larger Muslim representation in the provinces where Muslims were not in majority. It also agreed on a 33 percent Muslim representation in the Central Legislative Assembly.

Hardly three year later, the genocide at Jalyanwala Bagh on 13 April 1919, happened; hundreds of people were killed and several thousands were injured. All over the country, this act of the British government was condemned and protests were held all over the country. Such events further clarified that Muslims and Hindus cannot live under a Hindu majority rule.

The abolition of the *Khilafah* in 1924 was essentially a Muslim issue but the Indian Congress, particularly Maulana Abul Kalam Azad, fully exploited it to benefit Congress and to win Muslim following for Indian Congress. For Muslims, this was a watershed moment, they started to think like a nation but could not differentiate yet between Muslim nationalism and Islamic *millat* and *ummah* based on the Qur'anic concept of brotherhood and *jama'ah*.

At this point in history, Allama Iqbal emerged as an intellectual leader. He offered his criticism on the West and on the traditional concept of religion. His deep understanding of the Qur'an and love of the Prophet ﷺ, reflected in his poetry, inspired youth and a new consciousness *dawn*ed. The Khilafah movement earlier gave courage to Muslims to stand against the British rule. Now Iqbal called them to reconstruct their life on the basis of the Qur'an and the Prophetic example.

Iqbal knew well that the Muslim mind had gradually adjusted itself to the rule of kings and *sultans* with hereditary succession under Muslim dynasties. This no doubt was an obvious deviation from the model of *Khalafat-e-Rashidah*. But due to the coercive power of the Kings and the passive role of 'ullama, this *mulukiyat* was justified under the deceptive notion of "al-sultanu zillullah fil-ard" (the king is the shadow of Allah ﷻ on land). This was further reinforced by the non-political and passive role of the *sufiya*, which Iqbal strongly criticised.

Iqbal in his Allahabad presidential address to the All India Muslim League convention in 1930 made it very clear that the Qur'anic teaching of *tawhid* does not allow the acceptance of anyone as sovereign except Allah ﷻ. Therefore, for the Muslims of the subcontinent, there was no option. In order to practice their faith, they must have their independent homeland where Allah's Authority is realised. He rejected the doctrine of secularism in his address as an illogical and irrational concept because Allah's sovereignty simply means His Authority exists not only in the space of the masjid, but also in the market place, parliament, law courts, trade centre and even in playgrounds, and within the boundaries of home; in brief, in all possible human activities in a society. This was not possible under a secular state, even when not ruled by a Hindu majority. The concept of the nation state as such was contrary to the basic understanding of Islam as *din*, a way of life. *Tawhid*, he maintained, demands realisation of Allah's authority and sovereignty in all fields of life. Therefore, Islam cannot be properly practised in a society and state which believes in the dualism of separation between religion and state, or considers religion a personal matter.

The problem of the West and the so-called liberal Muslims has been, essentially, that they look on Islam as a religion, no different than how Christians, Hindus and others look on their religion. For followers of all other religions, religion means rituals, ceremonies, festivals and the development of a personal relation with their god, with whatever name they call Him. Worldly activities like trade and commerce and political governance are considered by them as secular. Iqbal, Asad, Jinnah and Mawdudi, all of them, reject this concept of religion as "personal faith" as foreign to Islam and contrary to the Qur'an and the Prophetic example. The Qur'an made it very clear that "All sovereignty (authority to govern) rests only with Allah. He has commanded that you serve none but Him. This is the Right Way of life (*al-din al-qaiyyim*)", Yusuf 12:40.

Needless to say, if Iqbal, Jinnah, Asad and others believed in a secular interpretation of religion as a personal matter between man and God, there was no logic in asking for a separate homeland. British colonialism guaranteed such religious liberty and the same could continue under a Hindu majority in an Indian secular democracy. Therefore, the basic dilemma of the secularist mind, Muslim as well as non-Muslim, has been blind faith in a dualistic world view of separation between a sacred and a profane space and time or separation between religion and state.

The second dilemma of the Westernised elite has been an obsession that an Islamic State means a theocratic state, because of their basic intellectual training in European history which reminded them of the theocratic rule of the Church in pre-democratic Europe. They failed to understand that an Islamic State by definition is not a state ruled by clerics or ordained and immune religious leaders. An Islamic state is a kind of its own, sui generis. The fact is Allama Iqbal, Allama Muhammad Asad, the Quaid and Maulana Mawdudi are on one page on the concept of the Islamic state as not theocratic.

The whole debate for over seventy eight years on what Pakistan's ideology and role of "religion" should be becomes irrelevant in the presence of the self-defining *statements* of the Father of the nation, his mentor Allama Iqbal and a close associate, Allama Muhammad Asad, documented in the following pages.

The so-called liberals knowingly or unknowingly in the past seventy seven years have repeated their own narrative as the history of the Pakistan movement. They grossly lack evidence in their assertions. This essay presents direct evidence in the form of authentic *statements*, speeches and writings of the founding fathers of Pakistan.

The apprehensions of liberals are not rooted in historical or conceptual foundations. Their main assumption is that, like other nation states, Pakistan was also created as a nation state, where Muslims may have economic gain and political power.

The discourse on what the ideology should be of a nation with an over 96% Muslim population, who sacrificed their all as the Quaid said for accomplishing a dream, appears a ridiculous question. But it has been raised so many times and so loudly that it appears a genuine issue. Unfortunately, the so-called liberal intellectuals and bureaucrats, who represent less than one percent of the country's population but who control the media in the country, have kept the nation in the dark about the intent and vision of the founding fathers including the Quaid, Allama Iqbal, Allama Asad, Liaquat Ali Khan, Nawab Bahadur Yar Jang, Sardar Nishter and the views of scholars like Syed Sulayman Nadvi, Maulana Shabbir Ahmad Uthmani, Maulana Mawdudi, Maulana Zafar Ansari, Hasrat Muhani and others.

They have always tried to confuse the issue by raising irrelevant issues like if Pakistan should be a theocratic state, which *fiqh* the state should follow, should we call the head of state *khalifah* or *amir* or president, can a female be head of state and so on.

They never bring to light that all these issues have been long settled by none other than the founding fathers. The authentic *statements* of the Quaid, Allama Iqbal, and Allama Asad in the following document show their consensus on these and other issues. To be specific, all of them declare that Pakistan shall be an Islamic state and not theocratic. They want to see economic development, modern education and strong national defence and unity based on the universal principles of the Qur'an and the Prophetic *Sunnah*.

With this backdrop, this essay makes an effort, not to interpret, but to directly refer to authentic and well documented *statements*, writings and speeches of Iqbal, Jinnah, Asad and Liaquat Ali Khan to speak for what they believed and not what we assume they believed.

This monograph offers direct access to the Quaid's vision, which was shrouded from the nation, in the name of liberalism and secularity of the Quaid. The least we can say about the covering up of truth and attributing to the Quaid what he never intended and said is that it is an intellectual dishonesty. It only betrays intolerance of the so-called liberals to listen to other than their own perceptions of the Quaid and Pakistan.

From community to *millat*, a faith-based entity

"Few individuals significantly alter the course of history. Fewer still modify the map of the world. Hardly anyone can be credited with creating a nation state. Mohammad Ali Jinnah did all three."[1] The fact is this compliment of Wolpert is an underestimation of the achievement of the Quaid. He not only achieved the above three goals, but he did more than the creation of a "nation state", as defined and understood in Western political thought. He rather replaced the concept of "nation state" with an *ideological* state where Muslims could fashion their lives according to their faith, values and culture. He made Muslims of the subcontinent rediscover their identity as *ummah* and a *millat*. The Quaid in very simple words elucidates on the nature of the constitution of this *millat*, new nation:

> *"What was it that kept the Muslims united as one man, and what was the bedrock and sheet anchor of the community," asked Mr. Jinnah. "Islam", he said, and added; "It is the Great Book Qur'an that is the sheet-anchor of Muslim India. I am sure that as we go on and on there will be more and more of Oneness-One God, One Book, One Qibla, One Prophet and One Nation".*[2]

The new *millat* the Quaid visualised was thus created and founded on its faith, Islam. The Quaid constructed the idea of Muslims in the subcontinent as a "religious minority" and demanded their recognition as a separate nation. To unify the Muslims, spread all over the subcontinent, in some place in small number and elsewhere in majority, in itself was no less than a miracle of the Quaid's leadership. Muslims lived in the neighbourhood of Hindus for centuries but their food, dress, language, culture, everything remained totally different. Muslims were beef eaters, while the cow was considered sacred and a deity in Hinduism. Muslims had their identity as a people of *tawhid,* Hindus believed in hundreds of gods and goddesses. Both communities had their own ways of life and cultures, founded on their respective faiths. This is why the Quaid summed up Muslim identity in only three meaningful words, Faith (*Iman*), Unity (*Ittihad*) and Discipline (*Tanzim*), as the motto of the new *millat.*[3]

Pakistanis as a nation are distinct. Their nationhood precedes the emergence of Pakistan as a state. They were born as a nation (*millat*) before Pakistan, as an *ideological* state, with a given territory and geopolitical entity that came into existence. It is this uniqueness of Pakistan which has not been properly comprehended by most Western historians, political scientists and liberal Muslim intellectuals.

Historical and political studies of Pakistan, by the Pakistani as well as other scholars, show a glaring incognisance of the *ideological* origin of Pakistan. This is perhaps due to their subscribing to the Eurocentric historical presuppositions. One among those is to interpret Pakistan's emergence due to purely economic and political considerations. Such presuppositions impinge on the research design, collection and classification of data, determining of historical stages and leads them to erroneously conclude that the Pakistan movement was perhaps inspired by the expected gain of economic and political power of the Muslim elite and entrepreneurs.

Most of the researchers' reliance on Eurocentric empirical social sciences research methodologies also leads them to recognise "religion" as one factor behind the Pakistan movement, but not as the core and the major motive behind the creation of Pakistan. They perceive Pakistan as a "nation state", which is totally the opposite of what the Quaid, Allama Iqbal and other founders of the nation visualised. These scholars often fail to see the substantial role of what they call "religion" in the emergence of Pakistani nationhood. Any involvement of religion in statecraft reminds them of "theocracy". Their basic assertion remains that religion should have no business with the state. Their academic and psychological presuppositions do not allow them to perceive the case of the Muslim struggle for a separate homeland in the subcontinent, for any other objective but economic prosperity. Their intellectual biases do not allow them to be objective and critical in their approach of the subject.

We believe that instead of a theoretical debate on whether Pakistan was conceived as a secular or an Islamic state, a more logical and down to earth approach may be to visit directly the vision of the founding fathers of Pakistan. For over seventy seven years, a one-sided narrative has been projected. There is a need to look directly into the speeches and public *statements* of the Founding Father and his associates. A brief review of the historical context may also help us to understand the context of the struggle for Pakistan.

The Muslim Community on the Eve of the Fall of *Khilafah*

The fall of the so-called "*uthmani khilfah*" in 1924 caused a great intellectual, political and psychological shock. It was a turning point in the intellectual history of Muslims in the twentieth century. It was, as it were, also a wake-up call for Muslim intellectuals. One great challenge was how to revive the khilafah. Muslim scholars were also led to search for the causes of the decline and disintegration of Ottoman power. Allama Shakib Arsalan, for example, tried to identify factors behind the decline of Muslim power. Allama Rashid Rida (1865-1935), on the other hand, tried to elaborate the meaning and historic need of the khilafah. At the same time, some intellectuals influenced by the European thought even questioned the very concept of khilafah in the Qur'an and the *Sunnah*. The Egyptian scholar Ali Abdel Raziq (1888-1966) represents this intellectual trend.

The intellectual climate in the subcontinent was not much different. Scholars and statesmen in the subcontinent came up with various responses. A group of the *ullama*, following a defensive and apologetic approach, thought Islam was in danger, therefore Islam can better be protected through the establishment of religious educational seminaries (*madaris-e-diniyah*). The emergence of seminaries at Deoband, Barailey, Saharanpur, Farangi Mahal of Lucknow and *Nadwatul 'ullama* as institutions represents this trend. Another sincere and serious pragmatic approach was to adopt the Western model of education, learn from the West and establish educational institutions on the pattern of Oxford and Cambridge in order to uplift the Muslim community. This resulted into the establishment of the Muhammadan Anglo Oriental College, later known as Aligarh Muslim University. The name of the institution clearly indicated its philosophy. Its major objective, perhaps was to primarily produce Muslim human resources needed to run the public administration of the British colonial rule in the subcontinent.

A third, rather optimistic, response came from Allama Muhammad Iqbal (1877-1938) who considered Islam as a comprehensive way of life, which had the potential capacity to change the political, social, educational and cultural decline of the Muslim *ummah* into a glorious future. All that was needed was to re-visit the original Islamic sources and revive the methodology of *ijtihad* or innovative thinking. He was followed by two of his contemporaries, Abul A'la Mawdudi (1903-1979) and Muhammad Asad (1900-1992), who, in one or another way, carried forward and complemented Iqbal's thought in their intellectual pursuits. The basic issues they addressed included what is the true nature of Islam, is it a "religion" in its Western meaning of the term or a comprehensive way of life, is Islam relevant to the so-called modern world, does it have a role in state and society and how to create an ideal Islamic society and governance on the pattern of al-Madinah.

European imperialism in the subcontinent concurrently was going through its own historical process of decay. The colonialists realised that with their military might, it was no more possible to continue their political control of the people in the subcontinent. The twentieth century became a century of global awakening for Muslims. Various political liberation movements emerged in the Muslim world. Their common concern was to free themselves from European imperialist hegemony over Muslim land.

The Indian National Congress, claiming to be the major political party of the country, presented itself as the main broker of liberation from the British colonialists. The All India Muslim League emerged as the representative body to protect the interests of over one hundred million Muslims of the subcontinent. It was not yet clear in the mind of the Muslim community what their ideal future political order should be. Even the leadership of the Muslim League believed for some time in Hindu-Muslim unity, as a strategy to get rid of a common enemy, the British colonial rule. For a while, they remained under the illusion that if certain religious and cultural rights of the Muslims were guaranteed, a confederation of autonomous Muslim and Hindu states could be a possible solution. But soon, several bitter political experiences taught Muslims that they cannot preserve their identity, faith and culture as a "religious minority" in a Hindu dominated secular parliamentary political system. They needed perhaps a state of their own or several autonomous states, but not a confederation under the hegemony of a Hindu majority rule.

At this point, a serious question emerged, do people living in the subcontinent constitute one Indian nation or are Muslims a separate nation? Allama Iqbal, Quaid-i-Azam Muhammad Ali Jinnah and Abul A'la Mawdudi claimed Muslims are a separate nation or *millat*. Therefore, they are two nations living in the subcontinent for centuries with their distinct historic, social and cultural heritage.

The Indian National Congress, on the other hand, claimed that all those who were born or raised in the Indian subcontinent were one Indian nation and the All India National Congress was their only genuine representative body; therefore when the British colonialists leave the country, it should inherit political power.

The concept of the nation state based on territory has been a known concept in Europe. The British, French, German and others justified their existence on the same principle. In Western political thought, the nation meant a people who may or may not subscribe to a faith but belong to a territory, race, language, ethnicity or colour. Faith for them was not the basis of nationhood.

The major contribution of Allama Iqbal, the Quaid and Maulana Mawdudi was to crystalise this concept of Muslims as a separate nation based on their faith and culture as the justification for the creation of an independent state. The Quaid knew well that with the concept of the nation state based on territory, Muslims could never liberate themselves from the tyranny of the Hindu majority.

The other core issue that attracted the attention of intellectuals was the nature of the future state. Should the new state follow the British type of parliamentary democracy? Does an Islamic state mean theocracy or rule of clerics, *'ullama* or graduates of *dini madaris*? What is the status of non-Muslims in an Islamic state? The founding fathers did not leave these issues undecided. The top leadership of the League including Allama Iqbal, Quaid-i-Azam Muhammad Ali Jinnah, Quaid *Millat* Liaquat Ali Khan and Bahadur Yar Jang were unanimous on Pakistan's ideology. However, a good number of the second rank of Muslim League leaders with feudal backgrounds and the British trained bureaucracy were at home with the idea of nation state continuation of the British parliamentary democracy, in which they were groomed. They thought the emergence of a new state is only a matter of a change of guards and not of the system.

The notion of Muslims as a separate nation logically implied the creation of an autonomous and separate state. The Quaid was fully convinced that Muslims as a nation cannot survive in a secular British type parliamentary system. He repeatedly said that in the given situation unless a separate homeland for Muslims is created, Muslims as well as Islam were bound to face a crisis of survival.

The choice for the Muslims of the subcontinent therefore was either to live as a religious minority in a Hindu-dominated secular British parliamentary democracy or to have a separate Islamic state guided by the principles of the Qur'an and the *Sunnah*. The concept of undivided India simply meant even when the Muslim population increases, the balance of power was to remain in the hands of Hindu fundamentalists or secularists. The concept of a secular India with a Hindu majority, the Quaid knew, was a contradiction in terms. The only logical way out, therefore, was to create a state where Islamic social justice, an Islamic economic system and Islamic political order could be realised.

It is also a fact that clarity of thought was missing in the second rank leadership of the Muslim League, the bureaucracy, judiciary and Western educated intelligentsia. The early death of the Quaid also left a huge gap between what he wanted and what the second rank leadership and later the army dictators tried to achieve.

Allama Iqbal's Vision of Pakistan

The first rank leadership of the League included persons like Allama Iqbal who, in his Allahabad presidential address of the All India Muslim League, very clearly touched on this vital issue. He underscored that Islam does not mean "religion" in its conventional meaning but is a total way of life. He further believed that Muslim majority areas may constitute autonomous states or units. For example, he mentioned that the North West, which included Kashmir, N.W.F.P., Punjab, Sind and Baluchistan, may form one unit of the Federation while East Bengal and Assam may form another unit of the Federation. Hyderabad, Jonagarh and other states where Muslims had a majority may also became autonomous states. His presidential address, in fact, carries a clear policy statement of the League. To avoid subjective interpretations, we have no choice but to quote a rather lengthy passage directly from Allama Iqbal:

> *"The conclusion to which Europe is consequently driven is that religion is a private affair of the individual and has nothing to do with what is called man's temporal life. Islam does not bifurcate the unity of man into an irreconcilable duality of spirit and matter, In Islam, God and the universe,*

spirit and matter, Church and State are organic to each other. Man is not the citizen of a profane world to be renounced in the interest of a world of spirit situated elsewhere. To Islam, matter is spirit realising itself in space and time. Europe uncritically accepted the duality of spirit and matter probably from Manichaean thought..."

He further elaborates that Islam means a way of life and not a religion in its Western connotation:

"What, then, is the problem and its implications? Is religion a private affair? Would you like to see Islam just a moral and political ideal, meeting the same fate in the world of Islam as Christianity has already met in Europe? Is it possible to retain Islam as an ethical ideal and to reject it as a polity in favour of national politics in which religious attitude is not permitted to play any part? This question becomes of special importance in India where the Muslims happen to be in a minority. The proposition that religion is a private individual experience is not surprising on the lips of a European..."

Allama Iqbal and the Quaid are on the same page in their understanding of Islam as not a personal religion but a total way of life with its own economic, political, social, legal and cultural system.

"The religious ideal of Islam, therefore, is organically related to the social order which it has created. The rejection of the one will eventually involve the rejection of the other. Therefore, the construction of the polity on national lines, if it means a displacement of the Islamic principle of solidarity, is simply unthinkable to a Muslim..."

Iqbal is fully in agreement with the Quaid on the future political order once the British colonialists leave the soil.

"The principle of European democracy cannot be applied to India without recognising the fact of communal groups. The Muslim demand for the creation of a Muslim India within India is, therefore, perfectly justified..."

"I would like to see the Punjab, North-West Frontier Province, Sind and Baluchistan amalgamated into a single State. Self-government within the British Empire, or without the British Empire, the formation of a consolidated North-West Indian Muslim State appears to me to be the final destiny of the Muslims, at least of North-West India..."

"I therefore demand the formation of a consolidated Muslim State in the best interests of India and Islam. For India, it means security and peace resulting from an internal balance of power; for Islam, an opportunity to rid itself of the stamp that Arabian imperialism was forced to give it, to mobilise its law, its education, its culture, and to bring them into closer contact with its own original spirit and with the spirit of modern times..."[4]

In his presidential address, Allama Iqbal made it clear that the Muslim League was not struggling for conventional "religious freedom" of Muslims, i.e., right to worship and celebrate certain festivals. This was not denied to them by the British nor could a Hindu-dominated rule deprive them of this human right.

The basic issue with the British and the Indian National Congress was that both believed in religion as a personal matter which had nothing to do with the state, while the one and only basis of the Muslim League for the creation of Pakistan was that it considers "religion" holistically; therefore political, social, economic and cultural activities draw their legitimacy from religious belief. Islam was not a religion but a way of life encompassing all possible human transactions in society. It was not a personal faith.

Allama Iqbal's concept of Muslim state was further reflected in his lectures, *The Reconstruction of Religious Thought in Islam*, and his philosophic poetry, in which he rejected the concept of the nation state; he called it a modern idolatry. Similarly, he rejected the idea of Western secular democracy as well as the rule of Church authorities or theocracy. He advocated the concept of Allah's sovereignty in place of the Western notion of sovereignty of the people. He advocated the use of modern institutional frameworks for fresh lawmaking. With his deep knowledge of Islam, he introduced the idea of collective ijtihad to be conducted by knowledgeable Muslims scholars in an elected parliament.

Is Islamic State Theocratic?

Allama Iqbal, Allama Asad, the Quaid as well as Maulana Mawdudi are on the same page on this vital issue: that there is no concept of theocracy in Islam and that an Islamic state by all means, is neither dictatorial nor monarchical or hereditary but a representative form of governance, as we will see later.

The Quaid, soon after the creation of Pakistan and in a post-11 August 1947 speech, in his radio address to the people of the U.S. in February 1948, expresses exactly same views:

> *"The constitution of Pakistan has yet to be framed by the Pakistan Constituent Assembly. I do not know what the ultimate shape of this constitution is going to be, but I am sure that it will be of a democratic type, embodying the essential principle of Islam. Today, they are as applicable in actual life as they were 1300 years ago. Islam and its idealism have taught us democracy. It has taught equality of men, justice and fair play to everybody. We are the inheritors of these glorious traditions and are fully alive to our responsibilities and obligations as framers of the future constitution of Pakistan. In any case, Pakistan is not going to be a theocratic*

state, to be ruled by priests with a divine mission. We have many non-Muslim, Hindus, Christians and Paresis but they are all Pakistanis. They will enjoy the same rights and privileges as any other citizens and will play their rightful part in the affairs of Pakistan."[5]

In this policy statement on the future constitution of Pakistan, the Quaid, as the head of state and as President of the Constituent Assembly of Pakistan, stresses three vital issues. First, the future constitution is to be based on Islamic principles which are applicable in life today as they were 1300 years ago. Second, the Islamic constitution and Islamic state do not mean theocracy or rule of the ordained clerics. Third, in Pakistan, as an Islamic state, non-Muslims shall be treated as equal citizens by the state.

The views of the Quaid on the nature of the future Islamic state as not theocratic have remarkable similarity with the concept of an Islamic state, elaborated by Maulana Abul A'la Mawdudi:

"By the word "vicegerency"(Khilafah), your mind should not turn towards the Divine Right of Kings, or to Papal authority. According to the Qur'an, the vicegerency of Allah is not the exclusive birthright of any individual or clan or class of people, it is the collective right of all those who accept and admit Allah's absolute sovereignty over themselves and adopt the Divine Code, conveyed through the Prophet, as the law above all laws and regulations. This concept of life makes the Islamic Khilafah a democracy, which, in essence and fundamentals, is the antithesis of the theocratic, the monarchical and the Papal form of government, as also of the present-day Western secular democracy"[6]

That an Islamic state does not mean theocratic rule is beautifully expressed by Allama M.Asad, a renowned Austrian-Pakistani Muslim scholar and Pakistan's first ambassador to the UN.

"Since every adult Muslim has the right to perform each and every religious function, no person or group can legitimately claim to possess any special sanctity by virtue of religious functions entrusted to them. Thus, the term "theocracy" as commonly understood in the West is entirely meaningless within the Islamic environment".[7]

The Quaid, Maulana Mawdudi and Allama Asad all three agree on the basic characteristics of the future constitution of the country, to be Islamic but not theocratic.

The Quaid in his earlier *statements* had criticised the modern Western or British parliamentary democracy. Then what was the vision of the founding father? Muhammad Asad who was commissioned to develop a blueprint of Islamic constitution, observes:

"... I do believe (and have believed for about fourteen years) that there is no future of Islam in India until Pakistan becomes a reality and that if it becomes a reality here, it might bring about a spiritual revolution in the whole Muslim world by proving it is possible to establish an ideological, Islamic polity in our times no less than it was possible thirteen hundred years ago. But ask yourselves: Are all leaders of the Pakistan movement and the intelligentsia which forms its spearhead quite serious in their avowals that Islam, and nothing but Islam, provides the ultimate inspiration of their struggle? Are they really aware of what it implies when they say the objective of Pakistan is la ilaha illa'Allah? Do we all mean the same when we talk and dream of Pakistan?[8]

We must remember Allama Asad is expressing these views in May 1947, in his journal *Arafat*, published from Lahore. There was no pressure of *'ullama* on him nor on the Quaid. Pakistan was about to be created. Muslim-Hindu conflict was at its peak. He, as a close associate of Allama Iqbal and the Quaid, did not belong to any so called maslki group of *'ullama* either. This shows the baselessness of the speculative claim of secular intellectuals that the concept of Pakistan as an Islamic state was an afterthought and a result of the *'ullama*'s pressure. It also contradicts the view that the objectives, resolution and declaration of Pakistan as an Islamic Republic was due to the pressure from the *'ullama*. We will see later what the Quaid himself said about Pakistan's ideology, which has been perhaps intentionally suppressed in historical and intellectual narratives on *ideology of Pakistan*.

Setting aside the myth that the idea of Pakistan was motivated by purely economic gains for Muslims, more specifically a project of rich Muslim *nawabs* and sardars and landlords to further increase their wealth, Allama Asad says:

> *"In the Pakistan movement, on the other hand, there undoubtedly exists such a direct connection between the people's attachments to Islam and their political aims. Rather more than that, the practical success of this movement is exclusively due to our people's passionate, if as yet inarticulate, desire to have a state in which the forms and objectives of government would be determined by the ideological imperatives of Islam – a state, that is, in which Islam would not be just a religious and cultural "label" of the people concerned, but the very goal and purpose of the state formation. And it goes without saying that an achievement of such an Islamic state – the first in the modern world – would revolutionise Muslim political thought everywhere and would probably inspire other Muslim peoples to strive toward similar ends; and so it might became a prelude to an Islamic reorientation in many parts of the world".*[9]

Voicing his reservations on the second rank of leadership of the Muslim League, Asad correctly observes:

> *"It is, thus, quite legitimate to say that the Pakistan movement contains a great promise for an Islamic revival, and as far as I can see, it offers almost the only hope of such a revival in a world that is rapidly slipping away from the ideals of Islam. But the hope is justified only so long as our leaders, and the masses with them, keep the true objective of Pakistan in view and do*

not yield to the temptation to regard their movement as just another of the many "national" movements so fashionable in the present day Muslim world, a danger which, I believe is very imminent".[10]

That the only objective of Pakistan's creation was the realisation of an Islamic state was crystal clear to the founding fathers of the nation:

"In short, it is the foremost duty of our political leaders to impress upon the masses that the objective of Pakistan is the establishment of a truly Islamic polity; and that this objective can never be attained unless every fighter for Pakistan – man or woman, great or small – honestly tries to come closer to Islam at every hour and every minute of his or her life that, in a world, only a good Muslim can be a good Pakistani".[11]

The fact is Asad's articulation of the Pakistan movement, as a prelude to a global revolution of Muslims, to inspire them to strive towards similar objectives, was understood more clearly by those who wanted to frustrate the idea of Pakistan as an ideal Islamic state. Their efforts were focused on confusing the issue and persuading the intellectuals to plead for a secular society. Asad could understand this better than those who were just Muslims by birth.

Later developments fully confirmed that the movement for liberation from British colonialism was led by persons, with few exceptions, who were themselves products of the British colonial epistemic and intellectual tradition. Moreover, in the first phase of the struggle, the leadership of the Muslim League itself was not clear on the issue of the future political map. They felt there was no harm in a strategic alliance of convenience between Muslims and Hindus. But soon, experiences in provincial elections convinced them this alliance of convenience cannot hold water for too long. Consequently, they had to part their ways as two separate major stakeholders in the freedom struggle.

Their common target though was to get rid of British colonialism. However, soon, political developments and ground realities convinced the

Muslim leadership that when the British leave the subcontinent, the political, legal, administrative and educational system they leave behind can never allow equal rights to the Muslim community. In the parliamentary system introduced by the British Raj, the Indian National Congress was the major beneficiary, Muslims were to remain always an ineffective, dependent and deprived religious minority with very fragile guaranteed safeguards to practise their ceremonies and rituals but not their *din*, values and culture.

The Muslims in the subcontinent knew well that observing "religion" in its European understanding as a "personal" and "private" matter for them was never an issue. Under the British rule, they were free to go to their *masajid* and the same was for the Hindu and Christian communities; they were free to go to their churches and temples. The issue was not the observance of "religion" as a private and personal matter. The issue was much deeper, how to run their economy, trade and finance in a *halal* manner, how to run governance under Allah's sovereignty, how to observe *'adl* and *salam* and mushawart or establish *khilafah* of Allah ﷻ on earth.

This dilemma of the Muslim mind in the subcontinent as well as in the Muslim world has been the main bottleneck and reason due to which the bureaucracy, political parties and legislative bodies, who always look West for guidance and believe in Western secular democratic and liberal ideas as their ideal, tried their best to avoid the introduction of an Islamic system in the country. Asad very correctly touches on this intellectual colonialism of Muslims:

> *"To a Muslim who takes Islam seriously, every political endeavour must, in the last resort, derive its sanctions from religion, just as religion can never remain aloof from politics: for the simple reason that Islam, being concerned not only with our spiritual development but with the manner of our physical, social and economic existence as well, is a "political" creed in the deepest, morally most compelling sense of this term. In other words, the Islamic religious aspect of our fight for Pakistan must be made predominant in all the appeals which Muslims leaders make to the Muslims masses.*

If this demand is neglected, our struggle cannot properly fulfil its historic mission".[12]

Being in close contact with the top leadership of the League, Asad was fully aware of the ground realities and the position taken by the Founding Father on Pakistan's ideology. He shows his full confidence in the sensitivity and commitment of the top leadership to Islam as Pakistan's ideology:

"The need for ideological, Islamic leadership on the part of our leaders is the paramount need of the day. That some of them – though by far not all, are really aware of their great responsibility in this respect is evident, for example, from the splendid convocation address which Liaquat Ali Khan, the Quaid-i-Azam's principal lieutenant, delivered at Aligarh a few months ago. In that address, he vividly stressed the fact that our movement drives its ultimate inspiration from the Holy Qur'an and that, therefore, the Islamic state at which we are aiming should derive its authority from the Shari'ah alone. Muhammad Ali Jinnah himself has spoken in a similar vein on many occasions. Such pronouncements, coming as they do from the highest levels of Muslim League leadership, go a long way to clarify the League's aims. But a clarification of aims is not enough. If these ideal aims are to have a practical effect on our politics, the High Command of the League should insist on a more concrete elaboration, by a competent body of our intellectual leaders, of the principles on which Pakistan should be built"[13]

Asad wrote this in May 1947 in the journal he edited from Lahore right on the eve of Pakistan's independence. His interaction with the Quaid and other top leadership of the league provided him first-hand knowledge of the ins and outs of the organisation as well as the thinking of the Muslim masses. He also knew well the mind of the Muslim bureaucracy and the so-called intellectuals who preferred to call themselves Muslims culturally or by birth and were hesitant in realising Islam in statecraft. His concerns coincide with the worries of the Quaid himself.

"It is quite possible that before these lines appear in print, the Quaid-i-Azam will have sent forth a call to the Muslim nation to establish a Constituent Assembly for Pakistan or if this has not been done so for, is bound to be done in the very near future. Hence, Muslim legislators and intellectuals must make up their minds here and now as to what sort of political structure, what sort of society, and what sort of national ideals they are going to postulate. The fundamental issue before them is simple enough; shall our state be just another symbol of the worldwide flight from religion, just one more of the many "Muslim" states in which Islam has no influence whatever on the community's social and political behaviour or shall it became the most exciting, the most glorious experiment in modern history: our first step on the road which the Greatest Man has pointed out to mankind? Shall Pakistan be only a means of "national" development of Muslims in certain areas of India, or shall it herald, all over the world, the majestic rebirth of Islam as practical political proposition?[14]

In his convocation address at Aligarh Muslim University on 16 February 1947, Asad referred to above, Liaquat Ali Khan made it clear that in Pakistan, sovereignty shall not belong to people or parliament but to Allah ﷻ.

"There is one very important question that will be asked. We say we want to live in our own way and in order to be able to do so we want to have a free and independent state. What is that way of life and what are the principles on which our state will be based? Such a question for a Muslim has only one answer. The ideal which Muslim has before him is and can be none other than the ideal that was set before the world by Muhammad P.B.U.H. of Arabia over 13 hundred years ago. The message that Muhammad P.B.U.H. brought is still with us, preserved for the whole of humanity in the greatest of all books, the Qur'an. Every Muslim should live and die for God. God is the only king, the only sovereign.

According to Islam, no one can wield authority in his own right as all authority is derived from God and can be exercised only on His behalf. Islam aims at building a society in which all possibilities of exploitation of man by man will disappear, in with all distinction of birth, colour and geographic origin will be wiped away."[15]

That Western democracy is not suitable for Muslims as a concept was crystal clear to the Quaid-i-Azam. He elaborated on it in his Aligarh University address on 6 March 1940:

"Two years ago, at Simla, I said that the democratic parliamentary system of government was unsuited to India. I was condemned everywhere in the Congress and press. I was told that I was guilty of disservice to Islam because Islam believes in democracy. So far as I have understood Islam, it does not advocate a democracy which would allow the majority of non-Muslims to decide the fate of the Muslims. We cannot accept a system of government in which the non-Muslims, merely by numerical majority, would rule and dominate us. The question was put to me, if I did not want democracy what then did I want fascism, nazism or totalitarianism? I say, what have these votaries, these champions of democracy done? They have kept sixty million people as untouchables; They have set up a system which is nothing but a Grand Fascist Council, their dictator (Gandhi) is not even a four anna member of Congress. They set up dummy ministries which were not responsible to the legislatures or the electorate but to a caucus of Mr. Gandhi's choosing. Then, generally speaking democracy has different patterns even in different countries in the West. Therefore, naturally I have reached the conclusion that in India where conditions are entirely different from those of the Western countries, the British party system of government and so-called democracy are absolutely unsuitable".[16]

As an experienced legal practitioner and a seasoned political leader who had personal experience of the British parliamentary system, the Quaid at this point in history appears convinced about the inappropriateness of the British parliamentary form of political system. The Quaid was fully aware of the global scenario in the late 1930's, the rise of fascism, socialism, and the decline of British colonialism was a writing on the wall. As a visionary leader, the Quaid opted neither for the British parliamentary system nor for fascism or socialism, but Islamic democracy and *Islamic social justice.*

The role of the *shari'ah* in the future order

In his conceptual development of how to protect interests of the Muslim *millat* in the subcontinent, Allama Iqbal played a very important role. In a letter he wrote to the Quaid on 28 May 1937, Allama Iqbal clearly indicates that only an Islamic *Shari'ah* based system of governance can solve the problems of the Muslims in the subcontinent.

> *"The Muslim has begun to feel that he has been going down and down during the last 200 years. Ordinarily, he believes that his poverty is due to Hindu moneylending or capitalism. The perception that it is equally due to foreign rule has not yet fully come to him. But it is bound to come. The atheistic socialism of Jawahrlal is not likely to receive much response from the Muslims. The question therefore is: how is it possible to solve the problem of Muslim poverty? And the whole future of the League depends on the League's activity to solve this question. If the League can give no such promises, I am sure the Muslim masses will remain indifferent to it as before.*
>
> *Happily, there is a solution in the enforcement of the law of Islam and its further development in the light of modern ideas. After a long and careful study of Islamic law, I have come to the conclusion that if this system of law is properly understood and applied, at least the right to subsistence is secured to everybody.*

But the enforcement and development of the Shari'ah of Islam is impossible in this country without a free state or states. This has been my honest conviction for many years and I still believe this to be only way to solve the problem of bread for Muslims as well as to secure a peaceful India. If such a thing is impossible in India the only other alternative is a civil war which, as a matter of fact, has been going on for some time in the shape of Hindu-Muslim riots.[17]

The Islamic order, the Prophet ﷺ, introduced in al-Madinah, as the point of reference, has been understood and interpreted differently by different people. The orientalists and their protégée consider Madinah as an outdated, "theocratic" model which cannot be replicated in a post-Christianity modern world. For the literal Muslims, it means the public implementation of a few *Shari'ah* punishments. For the so-called liberal enlightened persons, it means simply a historic evolutionary process, therefore the directives and commands given by the Qur'an and the *Sunnah* of the Prophet ﷺ in the seventh century need to be modified and updated. For revivalist thinkers like Iqbal and Mawdudi, the *Shari'ah* being divine and not a social construct is universal and to be approached holistically.

Legal punishments, no doubt, were introduced in a system of social, economic and political justice in which the Islamic state took care of welfare of its citizens. Even the state was responsible for a young person to get married and live a comfortable, responsible social life. Once human needs were fully met, a corrective and preventative legal system including punishments with full powers to the *qadi* (judge) who was authorised to determine the nature and level of an offence was a logical need. A *hadith* advised a judge to allow the benefit of doubt in forgiving instead of implementing a penalty. Allama Iqbal, Syed Mawdudi, Syed Sulayman Nadvi, Allama Asad and the Quaid represent this school of thought, as indicated clearly by Allama Iqbal in his above letter to the Quaid. The Founding Father, himself a legal practitioner, knew very well what Allama Iqbal meant by the implementation of Islamic *Shari'ah*. The Quaid himself refers to the *Shari'ah* when talking about Pakistan's constitution in his post-11 August 1947 address on Jan 25 1948 to the Bar in Karachi. The Quaid not only talks about his holistic view of Islam as a total system and that Islam is not a personal "religion", he reasserts Allama Iqbal's view that the new system shall be based on *Shari'ah*. And it has to be the basis of state and society in Pakistan.

The place of *Shari'ah* in statecraft

The Quaid specifically refers to the future constitution of Pakistan to be based on the *Shari'ah* in this address to the Bar in Karachi:

> "Quaid-i-Azam Muhammad Ali Jinnah, Governor General of Pakistan, speaking at a reception given to him on the Holy Prophet's Birthday by the Bar Association, Karachi, said that *"he could not understand a section of the people who deliberately wanted to create mischief and made propaganda that the constitution of Pakistan would not be made on the basis of Shari'ah."* The Quaid Azam said, *"Islamic principles today are as applicable to life as they were 1300 year ago..."*.
>
> *"Islam and its idealism have taught us democracy. Islam has taught us equality, justice and fair play to everybody. What reason is there for anyone to fear democracy, equality freedom on the highest standard of integrity and on the basis of fair play for everybody,"* Quaid-i-Azam Muhammad Ali Jinnah said, *"Let us make it (the future constitution of Pakistan), We shall make it and we will show it to the World"*.[18]

The implementation of *Shari'ah* for the Quaid and his mentor and advisor Allama Iqbal and Allama M. Asad meant the realisation of the sovereignty of Allah ﷻ in all walks of life, which was reconfirmed in the "objectives resolution" and in several of the Quaid addresses, and in speeches delivered by his associates, particularly Liaquat Ali Khan, Sardar Nishtar and Bahadur Yar Jang, on several occasions and in the Constituent Assembly of Pakistan.

Nawab Bahadur Yar Jang in his address to the All India Muslim League session in December 1943 made it very clear that the objective of Pakistan's creation was the realisation of Islamic ideology. The Quaid fully endorsed his views. Bahadur Yar Jang said:

> *"Gentlemen, the achievement of Pakistan is not as difficult as making it a true Pakistan and sustaining it. Your Quaid have, on several occasions mentioned that Muslims cannot frame their constitution and law by themselves. This constitution in the form of the Qur'an is already in their hands. How well taken is this vision and decision of ours? No one can deny the fact that we do not want Pakistan simply for the Muslims as a land where they become instruments of Shaytan and follow his track as done in so many other places in the world today. If this is the objective of our Pakistan, at least I am not in favour of such a Pakistan.*
>
> *Who can deny the fact that we want Pakistan in order to establish Qur'ani nizam hukumat.*
>
> *This will be a revolution. It will be a renaissance, a new life in which our cherished Islamic ideas and dreams shall become a reality and Islamic way of life shall be revived. If the constitutional and political system proposed by the planning committee does not have its foundations on the Book of Allah and the Sunnah of Rasool sallallahu alaihi wasallam, it will be a satanic political system, we seek Allah's protection from such politics."*

The Quaid banged forcefully on the table and said *"you are absolutely right"*.[19] Liaquat Ali Khan, as the first Prime Minster of Pakistan, while moving the Objectives Resolution in the Constituent Assembly, officially elaborated on the state policy on *ideological* issues. We have no choice but to make a rather long quote from him to set the record straight.

"Sir, I consider this to be a most important occasion in the life of this country, next in importance only to the achievement of independence, because by achieving independence we only won an opportunity of building up a country and its polity in accordance with our ideals. I would like to remind the House that the Father of the Nation, Quaid-i-Azam, gave expression to his feelings on this matter on many an occasion, and his views were endorsed by the nation in unmistakable terms. Pakistan was founded because they wanted to demonstrate to the world that Islam provides a panacea to the many diseases which have crept in to the life of humanity today".[20]

"We as Pakistanis are not ashamed of the fact that we are overwhelmingly Muslims and we believe that it is by adhering to our faith and ideals that we can make a genuine contribution to the welfare of the world. Therefore, Sir, you would notice that the Preamble of the Resolution deals with the frank and unequivocal recognition of the fact that all authority must be subservient to God. It is quite true that this is in direct contradiction to the Machiavellian ideas regarding a polity where spiritual and ethical values should play no part in the governance of the people and, therefore, it is also perhaps a little out of fashion to remind ourselves of the fact that the state should be an instrument of beneficence and not of evil. But we, the people of Pakistan, have the courage to believe firmly that all authority should be exercised in accordance with the standards laid down by Islam so that it may not be misused."[21]

"Sir, I just now said that the people are the real recipients of power. This naturally eliminates any danger of the establishment of a theocracy. It is true that, in its literal sense, theocracy means the government of God; in this sense, however, it is patent that the entire universe is a theocracy, for is there any corner in the entire creation where His authority does not exist? But in the technical sense, theocracy has come to mean a government by ordained priests who wield authority as being specially appointed by those who claim

to derive their rights from their sacerdotal position. I cannot emphasise the fact that such an idea is absolutely foreign to Islam.

Islam does not recognise either priesthood or any sacerdotal authority and, therefore, the question of a theocracy simply does not arise in Islam. If there are any who still use the word theocracy in the same breath as the polity of Pakistan, they are either labouring under a grave misapprehension, or indulging in mischievous propaganda.[22]

"You would notice, Sir, that the Objectives Resolution lays emphasis on the principles of democracy, freedom, equality, tolerance and social justice, and further defines them by saying that these principles should be observed in the constitution as they have been enunciated by Islam. It has been necessary to qualify these terms because they are generally used in a loose sense..."

"When we use the word democracy in the Islamic sense, it pervades all aspects of our life; it relates to our system of government and to our society with equal validity because one of the greatest contributions of Islam has been the idea of the equality of all men. Islam recognises no distinctions based upon race, colour or birth." [23]

"In the matter of social justice as well, Sir, I would point out that Islam has a distinct contribution to make. Islam envisages a society in which social justice means neither charity nor regimentation. Islamic social justice is based upon fundamental laws and concepts which guarantee to man a life free from want and rich in freedom. It is for this reason that the principles of democracy, freedom, equality, tolerance and social justice have been further defined by giving to them a meaning which, in our view, is deeper and wider than the usual connotation of these words."

"The next clause of the Resolution lays down that Muslims shall be enabled to order their lives, in the individual and collective spheres, in accordance

with the teachings and requirements of Islam as set out in the Holy Qur'an and the Sunnah. It is quite obvious that no non-Muslim should have any objection if Muslims are enabled to order their lives in accordance with the dictates of their religion."

"You would also notice, Sir, that the state is not to play the part of a neutral observer, wherein the Muslims may be merely free to profess and practice their religion, because such an attitude on the part of the state would be the very negation of the ideals which prompted the demand of Pakistan, and it is these ideals which should be the cornerstone of the State which we want to build. The state will create such conditions as are conducive to the building up of a truly Islamic society, which means that the State will have to play a positive part in this effort. You would remember, Sir, that the Quaid-i-Azam and other leaders of the Muslim League always made unequivocal declarations that the Muslims' demand for Pakistan was based upon the fact that the Muslims had a way of life and a code of conduct. They also reiterated the fact that Islam is not merely a relationship between the individual and his God, which should not, in any way, affect the working of the state. Indeed, Islam lays down specific directions for social behaviour and seeks to guide society in its attitude towards the problems which confront it from day to day. Islam is not just a matter of private belief and conduct. It expects its followers to build up a society for the purpose of "good life", as the Greeks would have called it, with this difference, that Islamic good life is essentially based upon spiritual values. For the purpose of emphasising these values and to give them validity, it will be necessary for the state to direct and guide the activities of the Muslims in such a manner as to bring about a new social order based upon the essential principles of Islam, including the principles of democracy, freedom, tolerance and social justice. These I mention merely by way of illustration because they do not exhaust the teachings of Islam as embodied in the Qur'an and the Sunnah. There can be no Muslim who does not believe that the word of God and the life of the Prophet are the basic sources of his inspiration. In these, there is

no difference of opinion amongst the Muslims and there is no sect in Islam which does not believe in their validity."

"Therefore, there should be no misconception in the mind of any sect which may be in a minority in Pakistan about the intentions of the state. The state will seek to create an Islamic society free from dissensions, but this does not mean that it would curb the freedom of any section of the Muslims in the matter of their beliefs. No sect, whether the majority or a minority, will be permitted to dictate to the others and, in their own internal matters and sectional beliefs, all sects shall be given the fullest possible latitude and freedom. Actually, we hope that the various sects will act in accordance with desire of the Prophet who said that the differences of opinion amongst his followers are a blessing. It is for us to make our differences a source of strength to Islam and Pakistan, not to exploit them for narrow interests which will weaken both Pakistan and Islam. Differences of opinion very often lead to cogent thinking and progress, but this happens only when they are not permitted to obscure our vision of the real goal, which is the service of Islam and the furtherance of its objects. It is, therefore, clear that this clause seeks to give the Muslims the opportunity that they have been seeking throughout these long decades of decadence and subjection, of finding freedom to set up a polity, which may prove to be a laboratory for the purpose of demonstrating to the world that Islam is not only a progressive force in the world, but it also provides remedies for many of the ills from which humanity has been suffering."[24]

"In our desire to build up an Islamic society, we have not ignored the rights of the non-Muslims. Indeed, it would have been un-Islamic to do so, and we would have been guilty of transgressing the dictates of our religion if we had tried to impinge upon the freedom of the minorities. In no way will they be hindered from professing or protecting their religion or developing their cultures. The history of the development of Islamic culture itself shows that cultures of minorities, who lived under the protection of Muslim states and

Empires, contributed to the richness of the heritage which the Muslims built up for themselves. I assure the minorities that we are fully conscious of the fact that if the minorities are able to make contribution to the sum total of human knowledge and thought, it will rebound to the credit of Pakistan and will enrich the life of the nation Therefore, the minorities may look forward, not only to a period of the fullest freedom, but also to an understanding and appreciation on the part of the majority which has always been such a mankind characteristic of Muslims throughout history".[25]

It is a strange phenomenon that historical facts, particularly what the Quaid and his right arm, the Secretary General of League and the first Prime Minister said repeatedly, has been totally absent even in the textbooks of Pakistan Studies. The only address of the Quaid in which he never used the word "secular", directly or indirectly – the August 11 presidential speech to the Constituent Assembly – is projected with a misguiding interpretation of his vision. We will talk about it later.

It is also necessary to remove a basic misgiving about the *Shari'ah* that it is a manifestation of the local Arabian tribal customs, punishments and penalties, culture and practices. The Qur'an at several places underscores that, in principle, all earlier *shara'ey* (pl. of *Shari'ah*) in their original form were revealed by Allah ﷻ and that these *shara'ey* follow certain universals, such as the sanctity of human life therefore, to kill a person unjustly is killing the whole of humankind (*al-Mai'dah 5:32; Isra 17:33*), or not to commit adultery (*al-Nur* 24:2), not to lie or falsely accuse a person (*al-Nur*24:4). Since all such commands in the earlier *Shari'ah* originate in one and the same source, the Divine *wahi*, or universal guidance, there was no need to replace all of them. However, with the passage of time, if certain commandments were altered, not properly preserved, forgotten or corrupted, their correction in later *Shari'ah* was a logical necessity. This is why the Islamic *Shari'ah* retained some and replaced other commandments. The Islamic *Shari'ah* never sanctified pre-Islamic Arabian tribal customs or social constructs of the seventh century.

The Islamic *Shari'ah*, it can be said with confidence, is not a matter of assigning normativity to the pre-Islamic Arabian customary law. The Islamic *Shari'ah* consists of universal divine principles and not the so-called local customs. The fact is that Islam came to Islamise Arabian society, law and governance. It never intended to Arabise the world. Therefore, a discourse on realisation of Islamic ideology, Islamic economic and political system is not only relevant but a logical need of the society, the state and people of Pakistan. This is why the Quaid on several occasions invariably repeated his vison and conviction about the constitution, social, economic and political order in Pakistan to follow the principles of Islamic *Shari'ah*, Islamic social justice and fairness. Allama Iqbal, in his Allahabad address, also touched on this aspect and said that when we create an Islamic Pakistan, we will distance ourselves from the "stamp of Arab imperialism" and develop our own legislation based on the Qur'an and the *Sunnah* of the final Messenger of Allah ﷺ.

The Quaid's Concept of Muslims as a (*millat*) Nation

The basic argument of the Indian National Congress, represented by Gandhi, Nehru, Maulana Azad and Maulana Hussain Ahmad Madani of Deoband, was that those who are born and raised in India are Indian and being Hindu or Muslim is their personal religious matter. This was also the official narrative of the British imperialists who were in favour of a united India, fully controlled by the Congress, when they leave the country.

The generalisation that the *'ullama* were opposed to Pakistan's creation based perhaps on the position taken by the Deoband also needs correction. It was the famous religious seminary *(madrasah)* of Deoband, represented by Maulana Hussain Ahmad Madani, which opposed the concept of two nations advocated by the Quaid and Allama Iqbal and validated by Maulana Mawdudi. The Quaid's position was that Muslims are a separate *millat* based on their religious, cultural, historical, literary, social, economic and legal tradition. Maulana Madani, as spokesperson of the one nation theory, wrote on the subject and tried to defend Jamiat 'Ulema-e-Hind's alliance with the Indian Congress. The only logical well-documented response, based on references from the Qur'an and Islamic sources, to the one nation theory of Deoband and Congress came from Maulana Abul A'la Mawdudi. This historical fact is completely overlooked when some intellectuals repeatedly make a totally unfounded statement that Maulana Abul A'la Mawdudi opposed Pakistan's creation. To elaborate on the idea that Muslims and Hindus are two nations, it was Mawdudi who, in 1939, wrote a booklet *Mas'ala-e-Qaumiyat*,[26] which provided the Muslim League with the authentic and only document that was widely circulated by the League all over India.

It was rather unfortunate that Maulana Hussain Ahmad Madani Shaikh ul Hadith of the recognised religious seminary at Deoband publicly opposed the concept of Muslims as a separate nation or *millat* based on their Islamic worldview, culture, history and faith. Another political group, the Ahrar, headed by Allama Inaytullah Mashriqi, also opposed the League's call for the creation of Pakistan and even used inappropriate language about the Quaid. A life attempt was also made by an Ahrari on the Quaid, which he narrowly escaped. This led to the creation of a misgiving that the *'ullama* opposed the Pakistan movement and even called the Quaid inappropriate words. Dr. Ishtiaq Hussain Qureshi, a renowned historian and veteran of Pakistan movement, observes:

> *"As the Congress ullama grew more unpopular, their writings became more and more vituperative ...The main target of their abuse was the Quaid -i-Azam, some of the maulavies drew special pleasure in distorting his name "Jinnah", an Arabic word, into jina and when this failed to irritate him or his followers, they assigned him all kind of insulting sobriquets like kafir-i-A'zam (this was invented by Ahrar leader Mazhar Ali Mazhar)"* He further adds: *The Ahrar ulema specially Maulana 'Ataullah Shah Bukhari and Habib-ur-Rehman Ludhianvi were strangers to a balanced language. They seldom mentioned the Quaid-i-Azam by his correct name".*[27]

It is a total distortion of history to say that the Quaid used his frequent references to Islam and Muslims simply for a political purpose. On the contrary, the Indian nationalist *ullama*, the Jamiat *Ulema-e-Hind* led by

Maulana Hussain Ahmad Madani, the Congress *Ullama*, who later enjoyed membership of Parliament and ministries in the Congress government, such as, Maulana Abul Kalam Azad, Hafiz Muhammad Ibrahim, Maulana Hifiz ur Rahman, Maulana Ahmad Saeed and Mufti Kifayatullah misinterpreted the Qur'an and *Sunnah* in support of the Indian Congress and kept claiming that "all those who lived in the subcontinent formed a nation.[28]

The rebuttal and response to Maulana Madani's *Mutahidah Qaumiyat aur Islam*, and the only scholarly elaboration of the two-nation theory, came from Maulana Syed Abul A'la Mawdudi. Dr. Qureshi comments:

> *"In fact, Maulana Mawdudi's rejoinder [to Mutahhidah qawmiyat aur Islam by Maulana Hussain Madani] was so logical, authoritative, polite and devastating that it was beyond the capacity of any supporter of a united nationhood to counter. Maulana Mawdudi pointed out that Maulana Hussain Ahmad had been carried away by his hatred of the British and had twisted history and facts. Are nations really created by political boundaries? If they are, why are ethnic, cultural and religious conflicts endemic in many states including the European countries? Maulana Hussain Ahmad had indulged in wilful distortion of the Arabic dictionary and even the meaning of verses of the Qur'an. He had no business to use a well-known word like "nation" in any sense except the one internationally assigned to it. The Muslims and Jews of Madinah did not form a single nation even after the Prophet had brought about an alliance between them for a short while after his migration from Makkah to that city".*[29]
>
> Dr. Qureshi continues:
>
> *"Maulana Mawdudi's superior scholarship, his telling arguments, his cold logic and his knowledge of modern concepts in political science and law made it impossible for the Jami'at group to answer his contentions. In fact, Mufti Kifayatullah, who was a faqih (jurist) and, therefore, more cognizant of the demands of logic and academic debate, advised his colleagues against*

any attempt to continue the discussion, because he opined that the Maulana Mawdudi was in the right and there was no point in attempting to defend the indefensible..."[30]

Dr. Qureshi's candid view, as a historian and participant in the Pakistan struggle and later a minister in the Muslim League government in Pakistan, exposes the myth of Maulana Mawdudi opposing the Pakistan struggle. He also documents that these were essentially the Deobandi and Ahrar "*ullama*", with their obvious alliance with Indian Congress, who were opposed to Pakistan's creation and the concept of two nation theory. The Deoband *ullama* who migrated to Pakistan tried to distance themselves from this guilt by spreading the unfounded blame on no one else but Syed Mawdudi, for opposing Pakistan, while he was the advocate of the two nation theory, which provided the Muslim League with real intellectual and authentic arguments for the Pakistan movement.

The undeniable contribution of the Quaid, however, remains his success in forgoing a "nation", *millat* based on Islam, prior to acquiring a political territory. This unique aspect of Pakistan's creation as an *ideological* state and Islam as the only basis of its existential reality as a nation, for unknown reasons, has been deliberately suppressed by a majority of intellectuals who write on emergence of Pakistan from a historical, political and economic perspective. This intellectual dilemma, if not dishonesty, in our view, is not confined to those who do research and write about Pakistan. It is an unconscious continuation of the Eurocentric colonialist intellectual tradition in social sciences which believes in the separation of "religion" and state. Any involvement of "religion" in statecraft by this mindset is considered theocracy, a notion Europe rejected in favour of the nation state. The Eurocentric mindset, founded on the presuppositions of the positivist and empirical research methodology, consequently, could find no substantive role of religion in statecraft.

If a textbook of political science teaches that politics and religion cannot mix, this presupposition influences the research design, collection of data, as well as the conclusions of a researcher. If a textbook in sociology defines man as a social animal, the whole study explores aspects of man's social behaviour with his basic "animality" as dominant factor when we study his behaviour in society. We understand and define civility, social conduct, normal and abnormal behaviour and socialisation as defined in the European paradigm of norms and values. Similarly, we assess and evaluate our economic development based on HDIs and benchmarks of modernity and civility developed and formulated by so-called experts from Europe and the US more recently. We decide our priorities and polices in the light of SDGs, a product of the Eurocentric mindset.

How can a student of history, who is made to believe that since the 16th century, Catholicism, or Christianity in general, has lost its relevance in political life, and, with the spectacles of positivism, believes religion a phenomena belonging to the age of mythology, therefore past and done, consider Islam as a faith which can be the basis of a nation and a state by replacing the concept of a "nation state"? Would it be logical for such an indoctrinated student of history to consider an *ideological* state, based on Islam, viable in the twenty-first century? And for argument's sake, if one believes it is possible, the only possibility this researcher will conceive will be a theocratic, fundamentalist sectarian *"talibanised"* state with no place for tolerance, moderation, pluralism and rational behaviour.

Our problem has always been continuation of our intellectual subjugation to the Eurocentric social science heritage. No political independence in the whole of the Muslim world has led to liberation from this deep-rooted intellectual slavery. We see truth as our former masters told us to perceive it. With all claims to freedom of thought, we never for once come out of the intellectual tradition in which we are born, grown and matured. Intellectually, we continue to live in the age of colonialism. Our political scientists and historians look on Muslim countries and the subcontinent in the context of a preconceived dogma of an ethnic, linguistic or religious minority struggling for its economic survival. They fail to think out of the box. In a post Sykes-Picot Muslim world, they only talk about nation states where "religion" is a personal matter, excluded from political arena.

The Quaid knew well that the movement of liberation from the British colonialists was not a war against the British in order to become slave to a known, visible and predominant Hindu majority. The Quaid was crystal clear on this. It took him sometime to discover this truth but once he understood the real mind of the Indian Congress, he made his position clear on both counts that Muslims in the subcontinent are not a minority but a *millat*, a nation and, second, that the so-called modern Western democratic parliamentary system is not suitable to Muslims in the subcontinent. It is a serious oversight, or rather a criminal negligence, on the part of Pakistani intellectuals to hide the real face of the Quaid from the people of the world for over seven decades. The Quaid made his position clear in his Aligarh address (6 March 1940) we quoted earlier.

The considered view of the Quaid that Islam has to be the basis of our political order did not change with time. All his post 1930 *statements*, speeches and addresses confirm his clarity of thought, candidness, honesty and integrity as a visionary and undisputed leader of the Muslims of the world. He not only condemned Western parliamentary democracy, in which he was at one time himself participating, but also made it clear that his ideal state is a new brand of democracy based on Islamic principles. This is a recurring theme in his *statements* and speeches which, again, have been completely neglected by most of the historians, political scientists and those dealing with Pakistan movement due to unknown reasons.

The position taken by the Quaid in an address in Bombay, even in 1943, was maintained and repeated on over a dozen occasions.

> *"The modern democratic form of government is not suitable to the genius of the Indian people... we want a true democracy in accordance with Islam and not a parliamentary government of the Western and Congress type."*[31]

The Quaid does not play with words; he conveys his firm commitment to a "true democracy in accordance with Islam". His straight forwardness, integrity and self-confidence never allowed him doublespeak. In his Bombay address, he further elaborated on the apprehensions of some people about an Islamic order. It is a common perception that Islamic rule means a monolithic political order, unfair and unjust to non-Muslims. No effort, though, is made to know directly from the Qur'an or the Prophetic practice as to how Islam looks toward non-Muslim citizens. The Qur'an explicitly states:

> *"There is no compulsion in din (religion). The right way stands clearly distinguished from wrong. Hence, he who rejects the evil ones and believes in Allah has truly grasped the firmest handhold which is forever unbreakable".*[32]

Elsewhere it further says:

> *"To you is your religion, and to me my way of life".*[33]

Muslim history, right from the time of the Prophet ﷺ, evidences the fact that the Islamic state and society has always been multi-religious, multicultural, multi-linguist and pluralistic. Knowing this fact, the Quaid in continuation of his address of 1943 says:

> *"In Pakistan, we shall have a state which will be run according to the principles of Islam. It will have its cultural, political and economic structure based on the principles of Islam. The non-Muslims need not fear because of this, for fullest justice will be done to them. They will have their full cultural, religious, political and economic rights safeguarded. As a matter of fact, they will be more safeguarded than in the present day so-called democratic parliamentary form of Government."*[34]

The Quaid here unequivocally talks about the future state of Pakistan which will be run according to the *"principles of Islam... it will have its cultural, political and economic systems based on principles of Islam".* In other words, Islam for him was not a matter of personal faith, worship, rituals, and ceremonies like Hinduism or Christianity define religion as a personal matter. He looks on Islam as a holistic system with its own political, cultural and economic principles and demands. Islam, as the state religion, therefore, makes the state responsible to implement Islamic political, economic and cultural teachings as clearly mandated in the Qur'an

> *"(Allah will certainly help) those who, were We to give them authority in land, will establish (the system of) salat, (the system of) zakah, enjoin which is good (ma'ruf) and stop evil (munkr)..."*[35]

If the Quaid really subscribed to the concept of religion as a "personal matter" and "religion" in his view had no business with it, then the fact remains that there was no danger to such "religion" under British colonialism nor under Hindu hegemony. Muslims could make their regular prayers in masajid, go for *hajj* and keep fasts. The real issue was not the freedom to go to the masjid or to go to churches and temples; it was the translation of Islamic teachings in political, economic and cultural life. Needless to say, an Islamic state never means the rule of a group of clergy, "*mulla*" or a theocratic rule. The *shi'i* concept of *wilayat-e-faqih* has not been endorsed by the four known interpretations of *fiqh*, nor an overwhelming majority of the *ummah*.

The Quaid's elaboration of Pakistan as an Islamic state in 1943, as quoted above, is totally overlooked by most of the so-called liberal, progressive Pakistani historians of the Pakistan movement. An objective and direct study, though, of his public *statements* speeches and messages validate what the Quaid said in 1943; it was maintained by him until he passed away.

The position taken by these historians and intellectuals is no different than the position taken by the *Jamiat Ulema-e-Hind*, represented by Deoband's Shaikh-ul-Hadith Maulana Hussain Ahmad Madani and well-known scholar Maulana Abul Kalam Azad; they believed Islam as "personal religion" which had nothing to do with state and concept of nation. Nationhood for them was based on territory and not on faith. Unfortunately, many Pakistani intellectuals, who could not detach themselves from the British colonialist approach, follow this theoretical framework of the Indian National Congress and Deoband in their assertions on the passive role of religion in a modern "Muslim" state. Religion is invariably considered by them as something personal and a dogma, with no role in public life.

The use of "Muslim state" in place of "Islamic state" also shows intellectual reservations of a number of Pakistani intellectuals. They think a country where Muslims are in 97 percent majority should be only a "Muslim state". Therefore, Pakistan, they think, was created to have a majority rule of Muslims. Again, this is a total deviation from what the Quaid invariably maintained, not once, but in dozens of his very clear, unambiguous statements.

A big intellectual gap exists at a conceptual level when we talk about Muslim dynasties on the one hand and the ideal Islamic state on the other. Most of these hereditary dynasties were monarchies, created in a total violation of Islamic principles of governance such as *shura, amanah, diyanah, ahliyah, ehtisab,* financial accountability and so on. Iqbal, Jinnah and Asad share a common vision of an Islamic state based on the Islamic principles of meritocracy, Allah consciousness, *amanah,* participatory decision making, *shura,* accountability, *ehtisab* and non-hereditary systems. The model Islamic state simply refers to the Prophet's ﷺ and the Khulafa al-Rashidun period. The later dynasties, commonly named as Islamic history, have never been taken by Muslim historians as ideal. On the other hand, all post *Khalifah* Rashid dynasties have been called a deviation from the Islamic concept of state.

The Pakistan movement took off in a political climate in which at least five noticeable responses to the British colonialism, or trends, can be traced in the subcontinent. First were the nationalist *ullama* of Deoband who believed in the one nation theory and were heralded by Maulana Abul Kalam Azad an *'alim,* a *mufassir,* yet a secular nationalist who later held the position of Congress President and Minister for Education in India. Other major nationalists leaders who publicly opposed the Pakistan movement included Abdul Ghafar Khan (Bacha Khan also known as Gandhi of Sarhad) and Deoband's Maulana Hussain Ahmad Madani. The nationalists believed that, on the basis of land, Muslims, Hindus and others were one nation, and religion was a personal matter. Even today, those who call themselves liberals in Pakistan firmly believe in this concept of religion.

This view was endorsed by the second stakeholders, the British imperialists, represented by the Governor General Lord Mountbatten, a cousin of the Crown, who fully aligned himself with the Indian Congress. British rulers, due to historic reasons, were not comfortable with the Muslims, from whom they took over the political power in the subcontinent. They had, on the other hand, a meaningful alliance with the Hindu leadership. This was evidenced when the announcement of independence was made in the Red Fort of Delhi. As reported by Dr. Ishtiaq Qureshi, thousands of people who assembled shouted "Pundit Mountbatten ki jai",[36] whom they considered their protector, mentor and benefactor.

The third stakeholders were the British trained bureaucracy, mostly products of Aligarh Muslim University, who firmly believed in the Eurocentric intellectual tradition in which the separation of state and religion was an article of faith. They had no idea about "Islamic democracy", "Islamic economy" or "Islamic culture". Trained in a totally secular, imperialist intellectual tradition, they could neither perceive nor think in a different way than their mentors. They were at home with European liberalism and so-called secularity and democracy. They proudly embraced the colonialist's system as a model of success. They always had a tendency to look West, which they thought was the source of ideas of liberty, freedom, humanity and democracy. Algerian thinker Malek Bennabi calls such a mindset a matter of "colonisibilty"[37] or a wilful welcoming of subjugation of the West, while an Algerian psychologist calls it the neo-colonial mind.[38]

The fourth stakeholder were common *'ullama* who, being product of *dini madaris,* were essentially interested in matters such as marriage and divorce, duration of *'ibadat* and controversial theological issues. Most of them confined their domain to *maslaki* issues and even regarded politics contrary to piety and religiosity.

Nevertheless, among them were also *ullama* who had political awareness and who supported the Pakistan movement with a clear understanding that Pakistan stands for *"la Ilaha illa Allah"*. Among them were Maulana

Shabir Ahmad Uthmani, Maulana Ashraf Ali Thanvi, Maulana Abdul Majid Badayuni, Maulana Syed Sulayman Nadvi and Abul A'la Mawdudi. Interestingly, the intellectual and *ideological* groundwork on the nature of an Islamic state and society was done mostly by Maulana Mawdudi. Though he had his reservations about the competence of the persons riding the bandwagon of the Muslim League, who in his view had serious deficiencies in the qualities needed to run an Islamic state he himself migrated to Pakistan before the independence of the country and played an active role in the rehabilitation of the displaced persons and refugees and remained in touch with the Quaid through his secretary Mr. Qamar Uddin Khan. He was also asked by the Quaid to deliver a series of lectures on the Islamic way of life on Radio Pakistan Lahore.[39]

This fourth group of *ullama* not only supported Pakistan movement, but tried to play an active role in the process of constitution-making with an Islamic perspective. One evidence of their vision of Pakistan can be seen in their unanimous twenty-two points[40] as guidelines for the Constituent Assembly of Pakistan. These *ullama* included representative of all schools of thought such as *Shi'a, Deobandi, Barelvi, Ahl-Hadith,* as well as non-denominational.[41] The twenty-two points, unanimously agreed by the *ullama,* cover basic issues that relate to the Islamic character of the constitution of Pakistan. Contrary to the common perception that the *ullama* can never agree among themselves, these representatives of all schools of thought, including *mashaikh,* had a consensus on the Islamic features of the future constitution of Pakistan, meaning of the *Shari'ah,* definition of a Muslim, and the nature of the state. These guiding principles reinforced the work undertaken by the Board of Islamic *Ta'limat* of the Constituent Assembly of Pakistan constituted by the Quaid. The creation of this cell in the Constitutional Assembly by the Quaid was also an indication of his concern for the role of Islam in governance and the popular support of the Islamic character of the country's constitution. Allama Asad, who was an active participant in the Pakistan movement, was appointed director of the National Bureau of Reconstruction at Lahore in order to propose guidelines for the future constitution of the Islamic state.

The Liberal Response

The secular elite in the country, due to their deep-rooted misconceptions about an Islamic state, however, continued their opposition to the Islamic nature of the constitution. Mostly on the pretext that the implementation of Islamic teachings will create hardship and violate the human rights of the around three percent religious minorities. The issue was never addressed on evidence-based research. The liberals and secularists always overlooked the fact that Pakistan was created on a clear mandate that it is going to be a country merely for Muslims, fully guided by the principles of the Qur'an and the Prophetic example as declared by the Quaid repeatedly. This was known to educated Muslims as well as to uneducated farmers labourers or non-Muslims.

Second, the mass population transfer provided full freedom to both Muslims who were living in places in undivided India, where there was a Hindu majority, and were expected to be controlled by Hindu secular democracy in India, to move to Pakistan. Similarly, those non-Muslims who were living in areas expected to become Pakistan had full freedom to move to India if they were of the view that it was difficult for them to survive in an Islamic state. Third, a sovereign state under all rational norms, with its 97%

Muslims population, by all democratic values and traditions and human rights norms, has a legal and moral right to follow its ideology in its political, cultural and economic matters. The state in such a situation shall have a moral and legal obligation to take the necessary steps for its citizens to live comfortably by their life vision and way of life. An over 97% majority is not supposed to be made hostage to the likes or dislikes of a 3% non-Muslim population. Therefore, the claim of the liberal intellectuals to follow the desires of the 3% population, i.e., to make country secular, by any democratic principles and human rights, cannot be considered logical or rational.

In order to support their view, the secularists and liberals tried to continuously misquote and misinterpret the vision of the Quaid. They claimed that the Quaid visualised Pakistan as a "secular state". An obvious truth they repeatedly overlooked was: did hundreds of thousands of men, women and children sacrifice their life, honour, properties and assets worth billions of rupees for a "secular state", with hope of just economic prosperity? Why could they not achieve their economic goals in a declared secular democracy in undivided India with a secular constitution and with a promise to the Muslims for their "religious" freedom? Was such a huge loss of life and property justified for purely economic gains of the *nawabs,* feudal lords and rich business leaders associated with the Muslim League? Was the Quaid playing with the religious emotions of the Muslims of the subcontinent to benefit some of his rich friends from the business community? Can even a non-Muslim opponent of the Quaid accept that he had two faces? Did the Quaid ever change the position he took in 1943 in his Bombay and in his 1945 statement in Peshawar, when he declared Pakistan to be an Islamic state? Did he, in the so-called 11 August 1947 speech, even use the word secular or separation of state and "religion"?

Did the Quaid Support Secularism?

The obsession, or rather a phobia of theocracy and the myth of secularity, has been a recurring theme in Pakistani academia and the print and electronic media dominated by the so-called liberal intellectuals, produced by the inherited colonial education system in Pakistan. Let us first try to explore the myth of secularity of the Quaid and try to understand directly in the light of the one and only statement he is claimed to have made in his interview to the reporter of Reuter Mr. Doon Campbell, in New Delhi, and later in his speech at the Constituent Assembly on 11 August 1947.

Justice Munir writes in his book *"the pattern of government which the Quaid –i–Azam had in mind was a secular democratic government. This is apparent from his interview which he gives to Mr. Doon Campbell, Reuter's correspondent in New Delhi in 1946, in the course of which he said:*

> *"The new state would be a modern democratic state with sovereignty resting in the people and the members of the new nation having equal rights of citizenship regardless of religion, caste or creed".*[42]

An excellent analysis of Munir's quote of the Quaid has been done by Saleena Karim of the U.K. in her outstanding research work, *Secular Jinnah and Pakistan: What the Nation Doesn't Know*[43]. It is shocking to learn that a senior member of the judiciary attributes such a statement to the founder of the country, putting in his mouth words the Quaid never uttered.

Saleena tells us that Justice Munir reports that this interview took place in 1946. Available authentic documents show it took place on 21 May 1947. The Quaid did not use the word "religion" in his response, he only mentioned caste and creed. The Quaid did not call the new state a "modern democratic state", nor did he make the people sovereign.

In her detailed analysis, Saleena tells us that the Munir quote indicates the Quaid used the words "the new state would be a modern democratic state, with sovereignty resting in the people and the members of the new nation having equal rights of citizenship regardless of religion, caste and creed" which carry a serious linguistic error not expected from the Quaid.

> *"...The new state would be a modern state" as such makes no sense. Normally we expect someone to say the "new state will be a modern democratic state."*[44]

What motivated Saleena to critically look into Munir's quotation of the Quaid was his citing the Quaid's statement in a conditional clause, without giving the condition. Such an error can never be expected from the Quaid. Furthermore, the typed responses of the Quaid to the question Doon raised, with corrections made by the Quaid along with his signatures, totally exposes the misreporting done by Munir.

Saleena writes "The date of the Reuter's interview of Jinnah with Doon Campbell provided by Munir was simply the year 1946. No proper reference was provided anywhere in the book. The actual date of this interview is 21 May 1947. The full transcript of the interview appears in the first volume of Z.H. Zaidi's Jinnah Papers. This, in turn, was obtained from an original typewritten document containing corrections in Jinnah's own handwriting as well as his signature, conforming the textual authority of this particular interview. The particular wording of the text as given by Munir does not appear in the interview".[45]

It is highly regrettable that a senior judge attributes to the founder of the country something fabricated, and then gives it a meaning of his own view that the Quaid wanted a secular modern democratic Pakistan. It is also worth noting that the Quaid never used the word "secular" in any of his speeches, *statements* or addresses throughout his life. Then what did he actually say? The document says:

> *"But the government of Pakistan can only be a popular representative and democratic form of government. Its parliament and cabinet, responsible to the parliament, will both be finally responsible to the electorate and the people in general without any distinction of caste, creed or sect, which will be the final deciding factor with regard to the policy and programme of the government that may be adopted from time to time"*[46]

> *"The question Doon Campbell asked was: on what basis will the central administration of Pakistan be set up? In other words, he wanted to know the thoughts of Jinnah regarding the nature of Pakistan. He wanted to know whether it would be a secular state or a religious state and how this would affect its relationship with neighbouring countries. It was an opportunity for Jinnah to call Pakistan a secular state if he chose, and this would have surely suited the Western audience for whose benefit the interview was being conducted".*[47]

The Quaid definitely did not say "the new state would be a modern democratic state" nor did he use the word "secular". The Quaid did not use the word "sovereignty" nor "modern democratic" nor the word "religion" either, in his typed written response. The Quaid in his response made it clear that the Constituent Assembly shall decide the final nature of policies and programmes of the government with mutual consultation or *shura*. It is unfortunate that what Munir falsely attributed to the Quaid in his book became the most authentic view of the Quaid. Munir has been widely quoted by Pakistani and Western writers as authentic evidence for the contention that the Quaid wanted a secular modern democracy in Pakistan.

The Myth of the 11 August 1947 allegation

Saleena Karim also refers to another important event in the same connection which provides an evidence-based contradiction of Munir and other liberal thinkers' thesis. On 13 July 1947, in a press conference at New Delhi, a correspondent asked.

"Question: *Will Pakistan be a secular or theocratic state?*

> Mr. Jinnah: *You are asking me a question that is absurd. I do not know what a theocratic state means.*
>
> A correspondent suggested *that a theocratic state meant a state where only a people of a particular religion, for example, Muslims, could be full citizens and non-Muslims would not be full citizens.*
>
> Mr. Jinnah: *Then it seems to me that what I have already stated is like throwing water on a duck's back (laughter). For goodness' sake, get out of your head the nonsense that is being talked about. What this theocratic state means I do not understand.*

Another correspondent suggested *that the questioner meant a state run by Maulanas.*

> Mr. Jinnah; *What about the government run by Pandits in Hindustan (laughter) when you talk of democracy. Mr. Jinnah went on "I am afraid you have not studied Islam. We learnt democracy thirteen centuries ago".*

The Governor General designate of Pakistan got up from the chair and, telling the correspondents that they had no more useful questions to ask, walked out of the room, But before he left a correspondent asked him: *I presume from what you have said Mr. Jinnah that Pakistan will be a modern democratic State. Mr. Jinnah quickly replied; "when did I ever say that? I never said anything to that effect."* [48]

Do we need to discuss his view on modern Western democracy when the issue was killed on the spot by the Quaid himself? Would that be a meaningful discourse?

Another most frequently quoted statement of the Quaid by liberal intellectuals is his 11 August 1947 speech when he took oath as President of the Constituent Assembly of Pakistan. It is claimed that, in this speech, he declared the separation between state and religion and that religion is a personal matter and has nothing to do with state!

Dr. Javid Iqbal helps us in understating the real context of the Quaid's statement:

"Islamic ideology recognises a distinction of meaning in the words "mazhab" and "din". "Mazhab" means personal faith, viewpoint or path, whereas din means a body of those universal principles of Islam which are applicable to entire humanity. Therefore, in this sense, Pakistan does not have any specific mazhab; because it is neither founded on nor projects the personal viewpoint of any particular Muslim sect. This very important aspect of the state of Pakistan was clarified by the Quaid-i-Azam in his famous Presidential address to the Constituent Assembly on 11 August 1947 when he proclaimed:

"You are free; you are free to go to your temples, you are free to go to your mosques or to any other place of worship in this state of Pakistan. You may belong to any religion or caste or creed that has nothing to do with the business of the state."[49]

Having said that, the Quaid illustrates his point using a familiar historical phenomena as an example. He refers to over two hundred years of bloody war between the two major sects (*mazahib*) of Christianity, the Catholics and the Protestants, killing each other just as the Muslims, Sikhs, and Hindus did during partition of the country. The Quaid continues:

> *"As you know, history shows that, in England, conditions, some time ago, were much worse than those prevailing in India today. The Roman Catholics and the Protestants persecuted each other. Even now, there are some states in existence where there are discriminations made and bars imposed against a particular class.*
>
> *The people of England in the course of time had to face the realities of the situation and had to discharge the responsibilities and burdens placed upon them by the government of their country and they went through that fire step by step.* ***Today, you might say with justice that***
>
> *Roman Catholics and Protestants do not exist; what exists now is that every man is a citizen, an equal citizen of Great Britain and they all are members of the nation. Now, I think we should keep that in front of us as our ideal and you will find that, in the course of time, Hindus would cease to be Hindus and Muslims would cease to be Muslims, not in the religious sense, because that is the personal faith of each individual, but in the political sense as citizens of the State.*[50]

It is obvious the Quaid is using "religion" or *mazhab* in its meaning of personal *fiqhi* interpretation, *maslak,* or sect, meaning Pakistan as a state shall not follow *mazhab* or *maslak hanfi, ja'fri, duobandi, ahl-i-hadith, maliki,* shafi' or any other interpretation but *Shari'ah,* i.e., the Qur'an and the *Sunnah* of the Prophet ﷺ, as he clearly mentioned in his speeches in Sibi and address to Bar in Karachi, both in 1948.

Unfortunately, Pakistani intellectuals and Western writers assume the 11 August 1947 speech was the only and perhaps the last statement made by the Quaid on the state of Pakistan. We have earlier seen in his address to the Hostel Parliament in Bombay on 1 February 1943:

> *"The modern democratic form of government is not suitable to the genius of the Indian people… we want a true democracy in accordance with Islam and not a parliamentary government of the Western and Congress type."*[51]

Another myth which has been often projected is that the text of the 11 August 1947 speech was kept in the dark by the bureaucracy and never highlighted. A simple question to be asked is why a bureaucracy obviously opposed to the introduction of Islam in state matters should suppress it, when it serves their purpose of making Pakistan a secular state. Moreover, the text has been available in practically over a dozen compilations of the *speeches and statements* of the Quaid including the book, Quaid-i-Azam Mohammad Ali Jinnah *speeches and statements*, published by the Ministry of Information, Government of Pakistan in 1989 with a signed forwarded by the then Prime Minister Benazir Bhutto.

The fact is, in this speech, the Quaid shares his serious concern about the after effects of the Hindu-Muslim riots during the partition. And to make his point clear that what he means by "religion" and citizenship, he refers to the historic fact of sectarian conflict between the Catholics and Protestants in the British Empire. We know well that until recently in the Northern Irish Republic, Catholics and Protestants were killing each other brutally. The same happened between Hindus and Muslims during the partition. He advises both to overcome that traumatic experience and learn to live as law abiding citizens like the Britons learnt through their experience. And, as the President of the Assembly, he assures minorities of the protection of their rights in this new state of Pakistan. Here again, he did not use the word "secular", yet some intellectuals obsessed with their love for secularity, try to read in between the lines what the Quaid never said, and then outrageously attribute secularity to him.

The real problem in our view is also hermeneutical. Western, as well as many Pakistani, intellectuals trained in the Eurocentric secular empirical paradigm of knowledge cannot conceive of a political order with a "religious" orientation. Their study of the history of Europe makes them believe that religion means dogmatism, superstition, hate and despotic rule of clerics who never use reason and logic and blindly follow the word of law, like the Baptist, Methodist and Presbyterian Christian fundamentalists. Their ideal of political order remains the British or American secular political set up. They fail to notice a dichotomy inherent in both the U.S. and British systems. Both claim to be secular, yet in Britain, only an Anglican can wear the crown and, in the U.S., the president invariably takes oath on the Bible and the one-dollar bill carries a religious confession that "we believe in God". This dichotomy is normal for people who believe in a dualistic view of life. For them, parliament and church both can coexist, one in a secular space, the other in a sacred space.

For Islam, as Iqbal mentions, Allah ﷻ has made all space a masjid, there is no secular world. State, economy, culture, law, social conduct everything is directed by the ethical teachings of the Qur'an and the *Sunnah*. State as well as economy and society have to be founded on the Qur'an and the *Sunnah*. This vital and substantial difference between the Islamic worldview and the Western secular worldview is not properly understood by our intellectuals, apparently due to their intellectual training in a Eurocentric epistemic tradition.

The point we want to bring home is not how Pakistani intellectuals conceptualise their own vision of Pakistan. As intellectuals they have all the liberty and right to advocate their own views. Academic freedom too requires respect of divergent views. We are concerned presently only with the ethics of research. It is unethical to put in the mouth of a person what he never said in his whole life. The 11 August 1947 speech of the Quaid is projected as his only public statement and perhaps his official will. While the fact is, in his pre-11 August 1947 and post 11 August *statements,* he clearly talks about his vision of Pakistan as an Islamic state. In his message on the 8 of September 1945, the Quaid refers to Islam as the basis of nationhood:

"The Musalmans are realising more and more their responsibility in every direction, every Musalman knows that the injunctions of the Qur'an are not confined to religious and moral duties. "From the Atlantic to the Ganges" says Gibbon "the Qur'an is acknowledged as the fundamental code not only of theology, but of civil and criminal jurisprudence, and the Laws which regulate the actions, and the property of mankind are governed by the immutable sanctions of the will of God." Everyone, except those who are ignorant, knows that the Qur'an is the general code of the Muslims. A religious, social, civil, commercial, military, judicial, criminal penal code; it regulates everything from the ceremonies of religion to those of daily life; from the salvation of the soul to the health of the body; from the rights of all to those of each individual; from morality to crime, from punishment here to that in the life to come, and our Prophet (s.a.w) has enjoined on us that every Musalman should possess a copy of the Qur'an and be his own priest. Therefore, Islam in not merely confined to the spiritual tenets and doctrines or rituals and ceremonies. It is a complete code regulating the whole Muslim society. Every department of life collective and individually."[52]

One can easily see the consistency in the thought process of the Quaid; he maintained one and the same vision of Pakistan as an *ideological* Islamic state and Islam as the holistic system or *din* and not as religion (*mazhab*) or a personal matter (*maslak*) in his earlier and later *statements* such as his address at the Hostel Parliament of Ismail Yusuf College, Bombay, as early as the 1 February 1943:

"In Pakistan, we shall have a state which will be run according to the principles of Islam. It will have its cultural, political and economic structure based on the principles of Islam. The non-Muslims need not fear because of this, for fullest justice will be done to them, they will have their full cultural, religious, political and economic rights safeguarded. As a matter of fact, they will be more safeguarded then in the present day so-called democratic parliamentary form of Government.[53]

It is worth noticing that whenever the Quaid refers to Islam, he further elaborates that it is not a matter of going to the masjid for prayer but Islam means "social, civil, commercial, military, judicial, criminal and personal code". Islam for him was never a personal matter as claimed by the so-called liberals. Going back to the early Prophetic encounter with the Arabs, historically, the problem of Makkans was not Islam as *mazhab*, but Islam as *din*. The secular and polytheistic society of Makka had accommodated over three hundred gods due to its religious pluralism. They had no problem in adding to their gods, Allah as a deity. But they knew accepting Allah ﷻ as Sovereign, Hakim, Malik, al-Aziz meant their economy, political system, cultural practices, moral standards, concept of time and space, in brief, everything shall have to change. Islam means a total way of life as the Quaid says again and again. It is this holistic view of Islam which could not be tolerated in a secular Hindu dominated polity. This was the only legitimate reason for the demand of Pakistan as an independent state so that the Muslims could fashion their lives according to their Islamic aspirations.

One major problem of Pakistani intellectuals, therefore, has also been lack of direct understanding of the Qur'anic concepts and terminology. The Arabic term *mazhab* is generally translated as religion in English language. Moreover, the Western and Eastern concept of religion is that it is a body of dogmas, rituals, ceremonies, festivals, offerings and invocations. Religion, therefore, in Europe and in India, meant personal faith as understood by those who claim to be religious. Islam, on the contrary, is more than what the term religion or *mazhab* or *maslak* means. Misunderstanding of Islam as *mazhab* or *maslak*, allows a person to jump to the conclusion that just as Christianity in the pre-modern West discouraged scientific investigation, opposed logical and critical thinking and imposed theological constructs on people in Europe through a theocratic state mechanism by the Catholic Church, similarly, an Islamic political order means a theocracy. Rule of *mulla*! Similarly, they perceive "religion" makes people sectarian and makes them hate and kill each other; therefore, religion should have no role in socio-political life. Islam, as *din*, and the Qur'an, as constitution, demands its followers to make the best use of reason, exploration into universe and the ethicalisation of individual, social, political, economic and cultural life — a total cognitive transformation, a paradigm shift. It is not a private relation between man and his god. *Din* is a totally different genre than religion.

These misgivings are founded on a preconceived stereotypical understanding of Islam as *mazhab* or religion. Islam calls itself *Din* in the Qur'an *"Indeed din in the sight of Allah is Islam"*[54]; *"This day I have perfected for you your din and have bestowed upon you My Bounty in full measure, and have been pleased to assign for you Islam as your din."*[55] *Din* in the Qur'an stands for a comprehensive or holistic way of life and is not limited to personal, spiritual relations with God or the offering of certain rituals and religious ceremonies.

If Islam really meant religion, it was already very safe under British colonialism, as very correctly said by Allama Iqbal *"Mulla ko jo hay Hind mein sajdey ki ijazat bechara samajhta hay ke Islam hay azad.* (Since *mulla,* in India, is free to make prostration in prayer, the simple fellow thinks Islam is free!) Muslims used to pray, go for *hajj*, pay *zakah* and keep fasts in *Ramadan* and go to their *masajid* under British colonial rule. Islam as "personal faith" or religion would have been equally safe even under a Hindu majority rule and perhaps is safe presently in this narrow sense in India, as perceived by some Indian Muslim intellectuals.

It is also necessary to know that *mazhab,* as used in Arabic, refers essentially to the well-known *fiqhi* interpretations such as *mazhab Ja'fari, mazhab* Hanbali, *mazhab* Hanafi *mazhab Maliki* or *mazhab* Shafi'i. It is in this sense that people call themselves, *salafi, ja'fari, Deobandi* or *baraelvi*. Neither the Qur'an nor the *hadith* ever call Islam *mazhab,* which is also an Arabic term, but only *din*. The Quaid did not consider Islam as *mazhab* but *din*. When we say Islam is the state religion of Pakistan in our constitution, we never mean Pakistan shall be a *Deobandi, baraelvi,* ahl Hadth or *ja'fari* state because the state has no religion (*mazhab-maslak*) but Islam as its *din*. The Quaid was clear on this point. This, he elaborates on one of his addresses:

"It is extremely difficult to appreciate why our Hindu friends fail to understand the real nature of Islam and Hinduism. They are not religions in the strict sense of the word, but are, in fact, different and distinct social orders, and it is a dream that the Hindus and Muslims can ever evolve a common nationality, and this misconception of one Indian nation has gone far beyond the limits and is the cause of most of your troubles and will lead India to destruction if we fail to revive our nation in time. The Hindus and Muslims belong to two different religious philosophies, social customs and literatures.

They neither intermarry nor interdine together and indeed they belong to two different civilisations which are based mainly on conflicting ideas and conceptions. Their aspects on life and of life are different. It is quite clear that Hindus and Musalmans derive their inspiration from different sources of history. They have different epics, different heroes and different episodes. Very often the hero of one is a foe on the other end, likewise their victories and defeats overlap. To yoke together two such nations under a single state, one as numerical minority and the other as a majority, must lead to growing discontent and the final destruction of any fabric that may be so built up for the government of such a state".[56]

In his written message to the Frontier Muslim Students Federation Conference Peshawar, 15 June 1945, he further elaborates on his vision of Islam as a comprehensive ideology and not a "religion" in its conventional sense:

"I have often made it clear that if Musalmans wish to live as honourable and respectable people, there is only one course open to them: fight for Pakistan, live for Pakistan, if necessary, die for the achievement of Pakistan or else Muslims and Islam are doomed.

There is only one course open to us to organise our nation, and it is by our own dint of arduous and sustained and determined efforts that we create strength and support our people not only to achieve our freedom and independence but to be able to maintain it and live according to Islamic ideals and principles. Pakistan not only means freedom and independence but the Muslim ideology, which has been preserved, what has come to us as a precious gift and treasure, and which, we hope, others will share with us.[57]

The specific use of "Muslim ideology" as the basis of freedom and independence by the Quaid further elaborates on his concept of Islam as a total system or way of life. This is why he again and again talks about "only one course open to Muslims" i.e., the creation of Pakistan or else he says "Muslims and Islam are doomed". The truth of his prophetic statement can be seen in secular India where not only Muslims but also Dalits, Christians, Sikhs and Buddhists are marginalised, though the constitution allows religious freedom to go to their churches, temples and stupas.

Concluding the Karachi session of the All India Muslim League, on 26 December 1943, the Quaid underscored the unique nature of Muslims as a nation. He pointed out that their nationhood was based on their faith in the Qur'an:

"What was it that kept the Muslims united as one man, and what is the bedrock and sheet anchor of the community, asked Mr. Jinnah. "Islam", he said and added, "It is the Great Book, the Qur'an, that is the sheet anchor of Muslim India. I am sure that as we go on and on, there will be more and more of oneness-one God, one Book, one Qibla, one Prophet and one Nation".[58]

The Quaid was crystal clear on Islam as the basis of nationhood, as well as on the meaning of Islam as a total way of life and not a "personal religion". He was not a person to accept any pressure from the *'ullama* either. His views on Islam were based on his own study of the Qur'an and Islamic law as a legal practitioner. Even before the creation of Pakistan, he speaks about the political and social role of Islam. He never considered Islam a personal matter.

"Everyone except those who are ignorant knows that the Qur'an is the general code of the Muslims. A religious, social, civil, commercial, military, judicial, criminal penal code. It regulates everything from ceremonies of religion to those of daily life... It is a complete code regulating the whole Muslim society in every development of life, collectively and individually."[59]

This shows us clearly that the Quaid never considered Islam as *mazhab* but as a total way of life. Therefore, his observations on *mazhab* on 11 August 1947 does not conflict with his persistent comprehensive understanding of Islam. It is in this sense he visualised Pakistan, not a sectarian Deobandi or *salafi* or *shi'i maslaki* state but an Islamic state. He did not consider Islam as a combination of rituals and ceremonies alone but a civilisational force. Perhaps this is why, while addressing the people of the U.S. on radio, he specifically calls Pakistan *"A Premier Islamic State."*[60]

That Pakistan's creation was necessary for the revival of Islam is another recurring theme in the Quaid's thought:

"We are a nation of 100 million of people inhabiting this great subcontinent and we have a great history and great past behind us. Let us prove worthy of it and bring about true renaissance of Islam and revive its glory and splendour".[61]

Similar views are expressed by him in his speech at annual conference of the Punjab Muslim Student Federation Lahore, 18 March 1944:

"The League had given them a definite goal and taken them out of darkness and confusion and give them a clear cut and crystalised goal of Pakistan which was now an article of faith with the Muslim, millions of whom were prepared to fight with their lives for its achievements. It was no more a slogan, it was something which the Muslims had to understand and in it lay their defiance, deliverance and destiny which would once more ring to the

world that there was a Muslim state which would revive the past glories of Islam. We want to rule our homeland and we shall rule"[62]

Islam, Islamic social justice and Islamic democracy remain his point of reference in his pre-partition, post-partition as well post 11 August 1947 *statements* and speeches. Just two months after his August 1947 speech, on 11 October 1947, the Quaid addressed civil and military officer at Khalqidina Hall, Karachi and elaborated on his vision of Pakistan:

> *"The establishment of Pakistan for which we have been striving for the last ten years is, by the grace of God, an established fact today, but the creation of a State of our own was means to an end and not the end in itself. The idea was that we should have a State in which we could live and breathe as free men and in which we could develop according to our own lights and culture and where the principles of Islamic social justice could find free play".*[63]

The Quaid repeatedly condemned Western liberal democracy and, with confidence, pleaded for Islamic democracy. On 14 February 1948, while addressing at Sibi Darbar in Balochistan, he reiterates his views:

> *"In proposing this scheme, I have had one undelaying principle in mind, the principle of Muslim democracy. It is my belief that our salvation lies in following the golden rules of conduct set for us by our great law-giver, the Prophet of Islam. Let us lay the foundation of our democracy on the basis of truly Islamic ideals and principles. Our Almighty has taught us that "our decisions in the affairs of the State shall be guided by discussion and consultation". (al-Shura 42:38).*[64]

One week later, on 21 February 1948, the Quaid addresses officers and the men of the Ack-Ack Regiment at Malir, Karachi, and again shares his vision of Pakistan in unambiguous clear words:

"You have fought many a battle on the far-flung fields of the globe to rid the world of the fascist menace and make it safe for democracy.

Now you have to stand guard over the development and maintenance of Islamic democracy, Islamic social justice and the equality of mankind in your own native soil. You will have to be alert, very alert, for the time for relaxation is not yet there. With faith, discipline and selfless devotion to duty, there is nothing worthwhile that you cannot achieve.[65]

He did not hesitate in naming the country an Islamic state much before the 1956 and 1973 constitutions of Pakistan declared the country an Islamic Republic.

"This Dominion which represents the fulfilment, in a certain measure, of the cherished goal of 100 million Muslim of this subcontinent, came into existence on 15 August 1947. Pakistan is the premier Islamic state and the fifth largest in the world."[66]

Some political leaders who were against the creation of Pakistan and were known supporters of the one nation theory of the Indian Congress did not feel comfortable on the persistent views of the Quaid on the Islamic basis of Pakistan and its future political and legal structure. They tried to create confusion and division in the country by spreading rumours and doubts. For example, one opponent of two nation theory and a known follower of Bacha Khan from the N.W.F.P. made a statement that Pakistan's constitution will not be based on *Shari'ah*. The Quai'd immediately took notice of it:

"Quaid-i-Azam Muhammad Ali Jinnah, Governor General of Pakistan, speaking at a reception given to him on the birthday of the Holy Prophet by the Bar Association Karachi, said:

"No doubt there are many people who do not quite appreciate when we talk of Islam. Islam is not only a set of rituals, traditions and spiritual

doctrines. Islam is also a code for every Muslim which regulates his life and his conduct even in politics and economics and the like. It is based on the highest principle of honour, integrity, fair play and justice for all." He further said that "he could not understand a section of the people who deliberately wanted to create mischief and made propaganda that the constitution of Pakistan would not be made on the basis of Shari'ah". The Quaid-I-Azam said *"the Islamic principles today are as applicable to life as they were 1300 years ago".*[67]

Perhaps only an intellectually colourblind person can say that after these continuous, post 11 August 1947, assertions on the Islamic nature of the state of Pakistan, the Quaid had a "secular" vision. He even used terms which, according to those Muslim intellectuals, who call themselves "post-Islamists", can easily brand him a fundamentalist, a supporter of "Muslim terrorism", if they only take time to read what he said in Lahore on the 30 October 1947, after his 11 August 1947 speech:

"Do not be overwhelmed by the enormity of the task. There is many an example in history of young nations building themselves up by sheer determination and force of character. You are made of sterling material and are second to none. Why should you also not succeed like many other, like your own forefathers. You have only to develop the spirit of the "Mujahids". You are a nation whose history is replete with people of wonderful gifts, character and heroism. Live up to your traditions and add to it another chapter of glory.

All I require of you now is that every one of us to whom this message reaches must vow to himself and be prepared to sacrifice his all, if necessary, in building up Pakistan as a bulwark of Islam and as one of the greatest nations whose ideal is peace within and peace without."[68]

The coherence and maturity of the thought and vision of the Quaid is remarkable. He is not a man of contradictions. What he held as his public view in 1943 and 1945, in his Bombay address, as quoted above, is fully reflected in his later *speeches and statements*. Another pre-partition statement elaborates on his vision he conveyed to the youth of the country as early as 1945:

> *"I have often made it clear that if Musalmans wish to live as honourable and respectable people, there is only one course open to them: fight for Pakistan, live for Pakistan, if necessary, die for the achievement of Pakistan or else Muslims and Islam are doomed.*
>
> *There is only one course open to us to organise our nation, and it is by our own dint of arduous and sustained and determined efforts that we create strength and support our people not only to achieve our freedom and independence but to be able to maintain it and live according to Islamic ideals and principles.*
>
> *Pakistan not only means freedom and independence but the Muslim ideology, which has to be preserved what has come to us as a precious gift and treasure and which, we hope, others will share with us."*[69]

These statements of the Quaid clearly indicate his vision of Pakistan as an ideal Islamic state. The hoax of Justice Munir that the Quaid wanted "a modern democratic state", in which sovereignty shall rest in the people and not belong to Allah ﷻ, has been already examined earlier. The honourable Justice very cleverly tried to mislead the people of Pakistan about the Quaid's vision and distort his personality. Depending on his unfounded statement about the Quaid, many Muslim and non-Muslim scholars tried to attribute a secular vision of Pakistan to the Quaid.

Historical and objective evidence in the above authentic *statements* of the Quaid contradict their views and perceptions of the personality of the Quaid. It is also totally unfounded that the Quaid's knowledge of Islam was not deep.

As a legal practitioner, he studied Islamic law and defended cases that needed deep knowledge of *shari'ah* law.

Contrary to what some intellectuals have been attributing to the Quaid, the available evidence, which has been, perhaps purposely, never highlighted in research works on the Quaid and in the textbooks of Pakistan studies and the history of Pakistan, shows a totally different vision of Pakistan. The Quaid consistently and coherently defined Pakistan as an Islamic state, and not a theocratic state because there is no concept of theocracy in Islam. This is exactly what Iqbal, Mawdudi and Asad maintain.

The Quaid was clear in his thinking that liberation from British colonialism meant the creation of a state for Muslims to translate Islam in their economy, society and state and make a departure from Western modern democracy. Steps to Islamise the system were taken in 1947 when a Board of Ta'limat Islami was created in the Constituent Assembly of Pakistan to guide the state. Later, in 1961, a statutory body known as the Council of Islamic Ideology, responsible to guide and continuously help the state in the socioeconomic, political and cultural implementation of Islam in the country, was created. It is unfortunate that the Council produced volumes of its recommendations that were never implemented by the self-centred and incompetent rulers who took over the country's leadership.

The Quaid on several occasions disapproved of British parliamentary democracy, which Pakistanis have considered as ideal; he, with equal force, questioned the capitalist world order. The following statement makes us believe that he could see ahead of time, the Wall Street crisis and the protests against the capitalist system in over one hundred business cites of world we observed in 2008.

Inaugurating the research wing of the State Bank of Pakistan, on the 1 of July 1948, just two months before he passed away, he said:

> *"I shall watch with keenness the work of your research organisation in evolving banking practices compatible with the Islamic ideals of social and economic life. The economic system of the West has created almost insolvable*

> *problems for humanity and to many of us it appears that only a miracle can save it from the disaster that is now facing the world ... The adoption of Western economic theory and practice will not help us in achieving our goal of creating a happy and contended people. We must work our destiny in our own way and prove to the world an economic system based on true Islamic concept of equality of mankind and social justice. We will thereby be fulfilling our mission as Muslims and giving to humanity the message of peace which alone can save it, and secure the welfare, happiness and prosperity of mankind".*[70]

Every single word the Quaid uses in his speeches and statement further cyrstalise his vision of Pakistan as an Islamic welfare state. He wanted a state "where principles of Islamic social justice could find fair play", he did not believe in Islam as a "personal religion". He is very clear that all aspects of public policy in Pakistan shall be governed and guided by the principle of *Islamic social justice.* The post 11 August 1947 statements of the Quaid are only a continuation of his earlier statements in which he talked about "Islamic democracy", "Islamic culture", "Islamic social justice" and the Islamic banking system.

The Name of the Country as its Identity

His commitment to Islam as Pakistan's ideology is also reflected in his public conversations. A historic event never told to the people of Pakistan relates to the name of the country. We know well that Chaudhry Rahmat Ali of Cambridge, U.K., along with his friends established a group of concerned Muslim youth in support of the Pakistan Movement. In 1933, he wrote a pamphlet, entitled "Now or Never, Are we to live or perish forever?" In this pamphlet he further developed the ideas of Allama Iqbal who, in his 1930 Allahabad address, proposed a Muslim state in the North-West of the subcontinent. Rahmat Ali coined the name of the country based on the first letters of the constituent parts of this proposed entity in the North-West of India. In his pamphlet, he proposed P for Punjab, A for Afghanistan, K for Kashmir and STN to represent Sindh and Balochistan. The proposed name therefore was PAKSTAN. We reproduce the covering letter of the pamphlet, along with the pamphlet at annexture III.

In 1940, the Muslim League held its session in Lahore in which, on 23 March 1940, what was later called the Pakistan Resolution was presented and passed. The next day, on 24 March 1940, Khawaja Abdul Rahim, an associate of Ch. Rahmat Ali at Cambridge, invited the Quaid and other leaders to tea at his Lahore residence. Sultan Zahoor Akhter reports the discussion:

> *"On March 24 1940, a day after the Lahore Resolution, Khawaja Abdurrahim, one of those who in Cambridge proposed the name of the country, invited the Quaid at his residence. The Quaid told him Rahim the name you gave in 1930 is highly talked about in Hindu press, Khawaja Rahim asked the Quaid then what should be the name in your view, Allama Iqbal in those days had already endorsed this name. The Quaid said "if you people and the Muslim nation like this name I have no objection, except in the name you have on the pamphlet PAKSTAN, add 'I' which stands for Islam and is the link between these provinces" Khawaja Rahim conveyed it to Chaudary Rahmat Ali, who was visiting Karachi those days.*[71]

This shows the mindset of the Quaid. It also shows that his real vision of Pakistan has been consciously misrepresented, distorted and suppressed due to a perhaps unknown fear of the Islamic *shari'ah* and a biased narrative projected repeatedly by so-called liberals. Consequently, history produced and taught during the past 70 years of Pakistan's existence has been biased, opinionated, one-sided and does not reflect the true mind of the founder.

The commitment of the Quaid to Islam and his clarity of vision was not an emotional or situational phenomenon. The above *statements* and speeches of the Quaid show coherence and continuity in his ideas, particularly his commitment to Islam as a way of life and, Islam as the basis of Pakistan and the believe that Islam is not a matter of "personal religion". In a public address to the All Indian Muslim League in 1939, he speaks his real mind:

> *"I have seen enough of the world and possess a lot of wealth. I have enjoyed all comforts of life. Now my only desire is to see the Muslims flourish and prosper as an independent community. I want to leave this world with a clean conscience and content with the feeling that Jinnah had not betrayed the cause of Islam and the Muslims. I do not want your praise nor any*

> *certificate. I only want that my heart, my conscience and my faith should prove at the time of my death that Jinnah died defending Islam and the cause of the Muslims. May my God testify that Jinnah lived and died as a Muslim fighting against the forces of "Kufar" and holding the flag of Islam high".*[72]

Needless to say, he was not a person who will doublespeak or who would like to win the sympathy of masses by such an emotional statement. The whole life of the Quaid is evidence to his clarity of thought, boldness, courage, integrity and straightforwardness. His cognitive part of the brain always prevailed over the emotional part of the brain. An undeniable piece of evidence of this aspect of his personality is another response when he was attacked by an Ahrari. A life attempt was made on him in his Bombay office by an Ahrari activist, which he narrowly escaped and was confined to bed when his daughter came to ask about his health. She knocked on the door of the room, The Quaid asked, 'Who is it?' She replied, 'It's me, your daughter.' His reply was "the presence of this person is more hurting than the injury". He did not change his position after denouncing her even in such an emotional situation. Indeed, he was a man of nerves, norms and principles. He was always guided by reason and not emotions.

The spiritual dimension of the Quaid's life is also totally neglected by his biographers. Maulana Hasrat Muhani, a known leader of the Muslim League, touches on this aspect:

> In 1945, Maulana Hasrat Muhani went to see the Quaid at his Delhi residence (10, Aurangzeb Road) and was told he does not like to meet people at this evening hour. It was time for Maghrib prayer, the Maulana prayed in the lawn, and then started walking in the corridor, He heard some whispers and thought the Quaid is talking with someone, he tried to peep into his room. What he saw was reported by him: *"The Quaid was sitting on the prayer rug and was praying to Allah for the success of the Muslims with tears and sobs".*[73]

Whenever the Quaid was asked a question about to which sect he belonged, his answer was one and same: Islam. We have no evidence of his following a sectarian approach. While in the UK or in the subcontinent he offered his Jumm'ah and Eid prayers with the masses in masjid in London, Lahore, Rawalpindi etc., with no protocols and like an ordinary Muslim.

That the Pakistan movement was inspired and motivated by Islam and has nothing to do with the European concept of the nation state was further reflected even in the oath of allegiance taken by the legislators of the League on 9-10 April 1946 at Delhi. The pledge does not begin in the name of democracy, motherland or liberty nor refers to champions of democracy in the West, it starts with:

> *"In the Name of Allah, the Beneficent the Merciful, then: Say My prayer, my sacrifice, my living and my dying are all for Allah, the Lord of the Worlds", al-An'am: 6:162* and ends on another Qur'anic dua: *"Our Lord! Bestow on us endurance and keep our steps firm and help us against the disbelieving people", al-Baqarah: 2:250.* The attached photocopy of the pledge signed by the Quaid is an other undeniable piece of evidence of the centrality of Islam in the struggle for Pakistan's creation. See Annex VI.[74]

The clarity of vision of the Quaid on the basis of the Pakistani nation is repeatedly reflected in his *statements,* as mentioned above. Before we end, we refer to Dr. Javid Iqbal, former Chief Justice of Lahore High Court, who summarises the Quaid's concept of Pakistaniyat, nationhood and citizenship.

> *"Consequently, the basis of nationhood in Pakistan is Islam. Islam acted as a nation-building force long before the establishment of Pakistan. Muslims gradually developed a national consciousness in the Indo-Pakistan subcontinent, they collectively struggled for the right of self-determination and the establishment of an independent homeland to be carved out from those territories where they constituted majorities. They eventually secured what they wanted.*

Hence, the historical fact which cannot be denied is that the formation of the Muslim nation preceded the demand for a country; on the contrary, the Muslim nation struggled for and brought Pakistan into being. Therefore, Pakistan is not technically the cause of any kind of nationhood. It is only an effect, a result or a fruit of the struggle of the Muslim nation for territorial specification".

He continues:

"Of course, we may now claim ourselves to be Pakistanis or belonging to the Pakistani nation but, strictly speaking, this is only for the purpose of identification among other nations of the world. Pakistani nationhood is not the real basis for the unity of the state of Pakistan; it is merely an apparent basis. At the present stage of our development as a nation, it is not a primary but only a secondary consideration; the primary being Islam, which cements us as a nation and also provides the basis for the unity of the state. However, the territoriality of Pakistan is not in conflict with Islam because, after its achievement there is no distinction between Muslim nationalism and Pakistani nationalism. They both mean one and the same thing. Even our claim on the territory of Kashmir rests on the same principle".

Dr. Javid Iqbal has a valid point on the concept of who is first, Islam or Pakistan.

"The same can be said respecting, patriotism, i.e., laying down one's life for one's country. Muslims do not have a notion of Pakistan as "fatherland" or "motherland". They may be attached to the geographical features of a country called Pakistan but they do not worship them. They are not prepared to lay down their lives manly for Pakistan's deserts, trees, mountains or rivers. This form of patriotism according to them is idolatrous. But, in their native soil, Muslims are ready and willing to lay down their lives for the religio-cultural principles on which the state of Pakistan is founded. Quaid-i-

Azam clearly illustrated these principles when he addressed the officers and men of the 5th Heavy Ack Ack and 6th Light Ack Ack regiment in Malir on 21 February 1948."

"You have fought many a battle on the far-flung fields of the globe to rid the world of the fascist menace and make it safe for democracy. Now you have to stand guard over the development and maintenance of Islamic democracy, Islamic social justice and the equality of mankind in your own native soil. You will have to be alert, very alert, for the time for relaxation is not yet there. With faith, discipline and selfless devotion to duty, there is nothing worthwhile that you cannot achieve". [75]

Dr. Javid Iqbal sums up the Quaid's concept of Pakistan:

"Hence, the first principle of the ideology of Pakistan as laid down by Quaid-i-Azam is that for Pakistan, Islam is the basis of their "nationalism" as well as "patriotism". But there is no room for sectarianism in Islam. Similarly, Pakistan is not expected to be a "theocratic" state because Islam is essentially a polity and aspires to create a civil society".[76]

This has been the spirit of Pakistan movement and the *raison d'être* of Pakistan's creation. We have miserably failed in transmitting this spirit and commitment to our younger generation who did not experience physically and emotionally the struggle their forefathers waged. We never used effective educational means of communication for this purpose. Our educational system and textbooks, parents and media have all failed miserably in the fulfilment of their responsibility. On the other hand, the Indian and secular lobby has fully exploited the available channels of communication to propagate the "one nation" theory of the Indian Congress and Deoband. They have actually re-written history with their biased and imported ideas during the past seventy eight years. It is time that truth be shared with the nation candidly with confidence, courage, objectivity and academic honesty.

It is amazing that several Pakistani and foreign scholars who study and write on the genesis of Pakistan fail to discover its real roots. But there are exceptions. One such exception is the Canadian scholar who taught at Aligarh Muslim University and Forman Christian College in Lahore, Pakistan, and was a first-hand witness to the Pakistan movement. He observes:

> *"A nation is not more Islamic than its people intend it to be. In the Pakistan case, on the other hand, these exponents contended, the whole raison d'être of the state was Islam: it was Islam that first brought it into being and that continued to give it meaning. The purpose of setting up the state was to enable Muslims here to take up once again the task of implementing their faith also in the political realm. The Objectives Resolution 1949 fired Muslim enthusiasm when it expressed such a purpose...Pakistan came into being as an Islamic state not because its form was ideal but because, or in so far as, its dynamic was idealist ... To set up an Islamic state was the beginning, not the end, of an adventure...To achieve an Islamic state was to attain not a form but a process."*[77]

Appendices

Appendix I

Twenty-two Points of the *'ullama*

1. ALLAH ﷻ is the REAL Sovereign and Lord of this universe.
2. The Law of the country shall be based on the Qur'an and *Sunnah* and no any law shall be enacted nor any Administrative injunction shall be laid down that is repugnant to the Qur'an and *Sunnah*.
3. This country shall not be based on any geographical, racial, linguistic or any other concepts but on those principles and aims which are based on the code of life laid down by Islam.
4. It shall be the obligation of the Islamic state to establish the goods defined by the Qur'an and *Sunnah*, suppress the wrongs and arrange for the revival and supremacy of Islamic beliefs and for the necessary education of established Islamic sects according to their understandings of religion.
5. It shall be the obligation of the Islamic state to strengthen the unity and brotherhood among all the Muslims of the world. It shall get rid of all the means that may give rise to differences among the Muslim citizens of the state due to ignorant prejudices of racism, linguistics, regionalism or any other sort of discrimination and ensure the stability of unity among the Islamic community.
6. The state shall sponsor, without any religious, race or other discrimination, the basic needs such as food, clothing, shelter, health and education for all

such people who cannot earn their livelihood or cannot do so temporarily due to unemployment, illness or other reasons.

7. Citizens of the country shall enjoy all the rights laid down for them in Islamic *Shari'ah*. It means protection of life, property and dignity within the law, freedom of religion and sect, freedom to worship, freedom of caste, freedom of expression, freedom to move, freedom to gather, freedom to earn a livelihood, equal opportunity to progress and the right to get benefits from social organisations.

8. None of the above-mentioned rights of any citizen shall be suppressed at any time without legitimate reason according to Islamic law and none shall be punished for any accusation of crime without the provision of an opportunity to defend and without a judicial decision.

9. The established Islamic sects shall enjoy complete religious freedom within the prescribed boundaries and law. They shall have the right to educate their followers on their religion. The decisions related to their personal affairs shall be made according to their religious jurisprudence and it shall be suitable to make an arrangement that their own judges make such decisions.

10. The non-Muslim citizens of the state shall enjoy complete freedom, within the prescribed boundaries and law, to practise their religion, worship, culture, religious education and they will have the right to get decisions on their personal affairs according to their religious law or traditions.

11. It shall be mandatory to abide by the agreements made with non-Muslim citizens of the state, within the boundaries of the *Shari'ah*. Both Muslim and non-Muslim citizens shall have equal civic rights as mentioned above in clause no. 7.

12. It shall be mandatory for the President of the country to be a male Muslim whose trustworthiness, capability and decision-making enjoys the confidence of people or their elected representatives.

13. The President of the state shall be responsible for administering the state. However, he can delegate any part of his authority to a person or an organisation.

14. The government of the President shall not be autocratic but consultative. It implies that he shall execute his duties after consultation with the members of government and the elected representatives of the people.

15. The President shall have no right to govern without the help of consultation after suspending the constitution partially or completely.

16. The organisation that shall elect the President shall also have the right to remove him with majority vote.

17. The President of the state shall have the same civil rights as general Muslims and shall not be immune to impeachment.

18. The same law shall be applied to the members and workers of the government and the citizens and the general courts shall implement it.

19. The judiciary shall be separate and independent from the administration so that the judiciary does not get influenced by the administration in performing its duties.

20. It shall be prohibited to preach or promote any such thoughts and ideologies which may be destructive to the basic principles of the Islamic state.

21. The various provinces and parts of the country shall be considered the administrative units of one state. Their status shall not be racial, linguistic or tribal entities but shall be of administrative territories, which may be delegated administrative authorities under the central dominion keeping in view the administrative convenience but they shall not have right to disintegrate from the centre.

22. Any interpretation of the Constitution that is against the Qur'an and *Sunnah* shall not be valid.

Appendix II

Names of the *'ullama* and *Mashaikh*

1. Allama Syed Sulayman Nadvi (Chairman of the Convention)
2. Maulana Syed Abul A'la Mawdudi (Ameer, Jamate-e-Islami Pakistan
3. Maulana Shams-ul-Haq Afghani (Minister for Education, State of Qalat)
4. Maulana Badar Alam (Ustaaz-ul-Hadees, Tando Allah Yar, Sindh)
5. Maulana Ihtisham-ul-Haq Thanwi (Administrator, Dar-ul-Uloom Al Islamia, Ashraf-Abad, Sindh)
6. Maulana Muhammad Abdul Hamid Qadri, Badayouni (President, Jamiat-Ulema Pakistan)
7. Mufti Muhammad Shafi (Member Board of Islamic Education, Constituent Assembly Pakistan)
8. Maulana Muhammad Idris Kandhalwi (Sheikh-ul-Jamia, Jamia Abbasiya, Bahawalpur)
9. Maulana Khair Muhammad (Administrator, Madrasa Khair-ul-Madaris, Multan city)
10. Maulana Mufti Muhammad Hassan (Administrator, Madrasa Ashrafiya, Neela Gumbad, Lahore)
11. Peer Sahab Muhammad Ameen-ul-Hasanaat (Manki Shareef, Sarhad)

12. Maulana Yusuf Binori (Shiekh-ul-Tafseer, Ashraf Abad, Sindh)
13. Haji Khadim-ul-Islam Muhammad Ameen (Al Mujahid-Abad, Peshawar) Khalifa Haji Tarang Zai
14. Qazi Abdul Samad Sarbaazi (Qazi Qalat, Balochistan)
15. Maulana Athar Ali (President Jamiat Ulema Islam, East Pakistan)
16. Maulana Abu Ja'far Muhammad Saleh (Ameer Hizbullah, East Pakistan)
17. Maulana Raghib Hassan (Vice President Jamiat Ulema Islam, East Pakistan)
18. Maulana Muhammad Habib-ur-Rehman (Sarseena Shareef, East Pakistan)
19. Maulana Muhammad Ali Jalandhri (Majlis Ihrar-e-Islam, Pakistan)
20. Maulana Dawud Ghaznavi (President Jamiat Ahl-e-Hadees, West Pakistan)
21. Mufti Jafar Hussein Mujtahid (Member Board of Islamic Education)
22. Mufti Hafiz Kifayat Hussein Mujtahid (Supreme Organization for Protection of Rights of Shia-e-Pakistan, Lahore)
23. Maulana Muhammad Ismail (Nazim Jamiat Ahl-e-Hadees, Gujranwala, Pakistan)
24. Maulana Habibullah (Jamia *Deeniya* Dar-ul-Huda, Therhy, Khairpur Mir)
25. Maulana Ahmad Ali (Ameer Anjuman Khuddam-ul-Deen Sheranwala Darwaza, Lahore)
26. Maulana Muhammad Sadiq (Administrator, Madrasa Mazhar-ul-Uloom, Khadda, Karachi)
27. Professor Abdul Khaliq (Member Board of Islamic Education)
28. Maulana Shams-ul-Haq Fareed Puri (Main Administrator, Madrasa Ashraf-ul-Uloom, Dhaka)
29. Maulana Mufti Sahab Dad (Madrasat-ul-Islam, Karachi, Sindh)
30. Maulana Muhammad Zafar Ahmad Ansari (Sec. Board of Islamic Education, Constituent Assembly, Pakistan)
31. Peer Sahab Muhammad Hashim Mujaddadi (Tando Sayeen Daad, Sindh)

Appendix III

NOW OR NEVER

Are we to live or perish for ever ?

By

CHOUDHARY RAHMAT ALI, M.A., LL.B., Barrister-at-Law
Founder, Pakistan National Movement

Published by
THE PAKISTAN NATIONAL MOVEMENT
Address in England. 16, Montague Road, Cambridge

3, MUMBERSTONE ROAD.

CAMBRIDGE.

28th January, 1933.

Dear Sir,

I am enclosing herewith an appeal on behalf of the thirty million Muslims of PAKSTAN, who live in the five Northern Units of India—Punjab, N.W.F.P. (Afghan Province), Kashmir, Sindh and Baluchistan, embodying their inexorable demand for the recognition of their separate national status, as distinct from the rest of India, by the grant of a separate Federal Constitution on social, religious, political and historical grounds.

May I venture to request you to acquaint me please with your valuable opinion as to the proposed solution of this great Indian problem as explained herein.

I do hope and trust that, vitally interested as you are in the permanent solution of this problem, the objects outlined in the appeal will meet with your fullest approval and active support.

Yours truly,

RAHMAT ALI,

(Choudhary).

ان الله لایغیرمابقوم حتی یغیروامابانفسهم

NOW OR NEVER

Are We to Live or Perish for Ever?

At this solemn hour in the history of India, when British and Indian statesmen are laying the foundations of a Federal Constitution for that land, we address this appeal to you, in the name of our common heritage, on behalf of our thirty million Muslim brethren who live in PAKSTAN—by which we mean the five Northern units of India, viz.: Punjab, North-West Frontier Province (Afghan Province), Kashmir, Sind and Baluchistan—for your sympathy and support in our grim and fateful struggle against political crucifixion and complete annihilation.

Our brave but voiceless nation is being sacrificed on the altar of Hindu Nationalism not only by the non-Muslims, but to the lasting disgrace of Islam, by our own so-called leaders, with reckless disregard to our future and in utter contempt of the teachings of history.

The Indian Muslim Delegation at the Round Table Conference have committed an inexcusable and prodigious blunder. They have submitted, in the name of Hindu Nationalism, to the perpetual subjection of the ill-starred Muslim nation. These leaders have already agreed, without any protest or demur and without any reservation, to a Constitution based on the principle of an All-India Federation. This, in essence, amounts to nothing less than signing the death-warrant of Islam and its future in India. In doing so, they have taken shelter behind the so-called Mandate from the community. But they forgot that suicidal Mandate was framed and formulated by their own hands. That Mandate was not the Mandate of the Muslims of India. Nations never give Mandates to their representatives to barter away their very soul; and men of conscience never accept such self-annihilating Mandates, if given—much less execute them. At a time of a crisis of this magnitude, the foremost duty of saving statesmanship is to give a fair, firm and fearless lead, which, alas, has been persistently denied to eighty millions of our so-religionists in India by our leaders during the last seventy-five years. These have been the years of false issues, of lost opportunities and of utter blindness to the most essential and urgent needs of the Muslim interests. Their policy has throughout been nerveless in action and subservient in attitude. They have all along been paralysed with fear and doubt, and have deliberately, time and again, sacrificed their political principles for the sake of opportunism and expediency. To do so even at this momentous juncture is a policy of Bedlam. It is idle for us not to look this tragic truth in the face. The tighter we shut our eyes, the harder that truth will hit us.

At this critical moment, when this tragedy is being enacted, permit us to appeal to you for your practical sympathy and active support for the demand of a separate Federation—a matter of life and death for the Muslims of India—as outlined and explained below.

India, constituted as it is at the present moment, is not the name of one single country ; nor the home of one single nation. It is, in fact, the designation of a State created for the first time in history, by the British. It includes peoples who have never previously formed part of India at any period of its history ; but who have, on the other hand, from the dawn of history till the advent of the British, possessed and retained distinct nationalities of their own.

In the five Northern Provinces of India, out of a total population of about forty millions, we, the Muslims, constitute about thirty millions. Our religion, culture, history, tradition, economic system, laws of inheritance, succession and marriage are basically and fundamentally different from those of the people living in the rest of India. The ideals which move our thirty million brethren-in-faith living in these Provinces to make the highest sacrifices are fundamentally different from those which inspire the Hindus. These differences are not confined to the broad basic principles—far from it. They extend to the minutest details of our lives. We do not inter-dine; we do not inter-marry. Our national customs and calendars, even our diet and dress are different.

It is preposterous to compare, as some superficial observers do, the differences between Muslims and Hindus with those between Roman Catholics and Protestants. Both the Catholics and Protestants are part and parcel of one religious system—Christianity; while the Hindus and Muslim are the followers of two essentially and fundamentally different religious systems. Religion in the case of Muslims and Hindus is not a matter of private opinion as it is in the case of Christians; but on the other hand constitutes a Civic Church which lays down a code of conduct to be observed by their adherents from birth to death.

If we, the Muslims of Pakstan, with our distinct marks of nationality, are deluded into the proposed Indian Federation by friends or foes, we are reduced to a minority of one to four. It is this which sounds the death-knell of the Muslim nation in India for ever. To realise the full magnitude of this impending catastrophe, let us remind you that we thirty millions constitute about one-tenth of the whole Muslim world. The total area of the five units comprising PAKISTAN, which are our homelands, is four times that of Italy, three times that of Germany and twice that of France; and our population seven times that of the Commonwealth of Australia, four times that of the Dominion of Canada, twice that of Spain, and equal to France and Italy considered individually.

These are facts—hard facts and realities—which we challenge anybody to contradict. It is on the basis of these facts that we make bold to assert without the least fear of contradiction that we, Muslims of PAKISTAN, do possess a separate and distinct nationality from the rest of India, where the Hindu nation lives and has every right to live. We, therefore, deserve and must demand the recognition of a separate national status by the grant of a separate Federal Constitution from the rest of India.

In addressing this appeal to the Muslims of India, we are also addressing it to the two other great interests—British and Hindu—involved in the settlement of India's future. They must understand that in our conviction our body and soul are at stake. Our very being and well-being depends upon it. For our five great Northern states to join an All-India Federation would be disastrous, not only to ourselves, but to every other race and interest in India, including the British and the Hindu.

This is more especially true when there is a just and reasonable alternative to the proposed settlement, which will lay the foundations of a peaceful future for this great sub-continent; and should certainly allow of the highest development of each of these two peoples without one being subject to another. This alternative is a separate Federation of these five predominantly Muslim units—Punjab, North-West Frontier Province (Afghan Province), Kashmir, Sind and Baluchistan. The Muslim Federation of North-West India would provide the bulwark of a buffer state against any invasion either of ideas or of arms from outside. The creation of such a federation would not materially disturb the ratio of the Muslim and Hindu population in the rest of India. It is wholly to the interest of British and Hindu statesmanship to have as an ally a free, powerful and contented Muslim nation having a similar but separate Constitution to that which is being enacted for the rest of India. Nothing but a separate Federation of our homelands would satisfy us. This demand is basically different from the suggestion put forward by Doctor Sir Muhammad Iqbal in his Presidential address to the All-India Muslim League in 1930. While he proposed the amalgamation of these Provinces into a single state forming a unit of the All-India Federation, we propose that these Provinces should have a separate Federation of their own. There can be no peace and tranquillity in the land if we, the Muslims, are duped into a Hindu-dominated Federation where we cannot be the masters of our own destiny and captains of our own souls.

Do the safeguards provided for in the Constitution give us any scope to work for our salvation along our own lines? Not a bit. Safeguard is the magic word which holds our leaders spellbound, and has dulled their consciences. In the ecstasy of their hallucinations they think that the pills of safeguards can cure nation-annihilating earthquakes. Safeguards asked for by these leaders and agreed to by the makers of the Constitution can never be a substitute for the loss of separate nationality. We, the Muslims, shall have to fight that course of suicidal insanity to death. What safeguards can be devised to prevent our minority of one in four in an All-India Federation from being sacrificed on every vital issue to the aims and interests of the majority race, which differs from us in every essential of individual and corporate life? What safeguards can prevent the catastrophe of the Muslim nation smarting and suffering eternally at the frustration of its every social and religious ideal? What safeguards can compensate our nation awakened to its national consciousness for the destruction of its distinct national status? However, effective and extensive the safeguards may be, the vital organs and proud symbols of our national life, such as army and navy, foreign relations, trade and commerce, communications, posts and telegraphs, taxation and customs, will not be under our control, but will be in the hands of a Federal Government, which is bound to be overwhelmingly Hindu. With all this, how can we, the Muslims, achieve any of our ideals if those ideals conflict—conflict as they must—with the ideals of Hindus?

The history of the last century, in this respect, is full of unforgettable lessons for us. Even one who runs may read them. To take just one instance: Despite all these safeguards and guarantees we have enjoyed in the past, the very name of our national language—URDU, even now the *lingua franca* of that great sub-continent—has been wiped out of the list of Indian languages. We have just to open the latest census report to verify it. This by itself is a tragic fall. Are we fated to fall farther? But that too is dust in the scales by comparison with the tremendous national issues involving our whole future as a nation and a power not only in India but also in the whole of Asia.

In the face of these incontrovertible facts, we are entitled to ask for what purpose are we being asked to make the supreme sacrifice of surrendering our nationality and submitting ourselves and our posterity to Non-Muslim domination? What good is likely to accrue to Islam and Muslims by going into the Federation is a thing which passes our understanding. Are we to be crucified just to save the faces of our leaders, or to bolster up the preposterous falsehood that India can be a single nation? Is it with a view to achieve [sic.] a compromise at all costs, or is it to support the illusion that Hindu nationalism is working in the interests of Muslims as well as Hindus? Irony is flattered to death by a mental muddle of such a nature and on such a scale. We have suffered in the past without a murmur and faced dangers without demur. The one thing we would never suffer is our own self-strangulation. We will not crucify ourselves upon the cross of Hindu nationalism in order to make a Hindu-holiday.

May we be permitted to ask of all those statesmen—Muslim or British or Hindu—supporting the Federal Constitution, if it is really desirable to make our nation sacrifice all that Islam has given us during the last fourteen hundred years to make India a nation? Does humanity really stand to gain by this stupendous sacrifice? We dare say that still in Islam the ancient fire glows and promises much for the future, if only the leaders would let it live. Whilst in Europe, excluding Russia, in about the same area as that of India and with about the same population, there live and prosper as many as twenty-six nations, with one and the same religion, civilisation and economic system, surely it is not only possible but highly desirable for two fundamentally different and distinct nations, i.e., Muslim and Hindu, to live as friendly neighbours in peace and prosperity in that vast sub-continent. What bitter irony is it that our leaders have not the courage to stand up and demand the minimum for our political salvation.

We are face to face with a first-rate tragedy, the like of which has not been seen even in the long and eventful history of Islam. It is not the question of a sect or of a community going down; but it is the supreme problem which affects the destiny of the whole of Islam and the millions of human beings who, till quite recently, were the custodians of the glory of Islam in India and the defenders of its frontiers. We have a still greater future before us, if only our soul can be saved from the perpetual bondage of slavery forged in an All-India Federation. Let us make no mistake about it. The issue is now or never. Either we live or perish for ever. The future is ours only if we live up to our faith. It does not lie in the lap of the gods, but it rests in our own hands. We can make or mar it. The history of the last century is full of open warnings, and they are as plain as were ever given to any nation. Shall it be said of us that we ignored all these warnings and allowed our ancient heritage to perish in our own hands?

MOHD ASLAM KHAN,
(Khattak).
President, Khyber Union.

RAHMAT ALI,
(Choudhary).

SHEIKH MOHD SADIQ,
(Sahibzada).

INAYAT ULLAH KHAN,
(of Charsaddah).
Secretary, Khyber Union.

Appendix IV

WHAT DO WE MEAN BY PAKISTAN?

By Allama Muhammad Asad*

كُنْتُمْ خَيرُ أُمَّةٍ أُخْرِجَتْ لِلنَّاسِ تَأْمُرُوْنَ بِالْمَعْرُوْفِ وَتَنْهَوْنَ عَنِ الْمُنْكَرِ وَتُؤْمِنُوْنَ بِاللهِ

"You are the best community that has been sent forth to mankind: for you enjoin Right and forbid Wrong and have faith in God". (*Al-Imran* 3: 110)

Looking at Ourselves

Some time ago—in the February issue of *Arafat*—I posed the question, "Do we really want Islam?" It was not just a rhetorical question meant for my readers' edification, but one which we must actually ask ourselves: and the time has come when every one of us must face it squarely, examine all its implications with regard to our present and our future, and summon the moral courage to answer it with an honest yes or an equally honest no. As things stand at present, innumerable Muslims say yes with their lips and no with their actions: that is, they frequently talk of Islam and assert, with all the marks of deep-set conviction, that it is the best possible way of life—the *only* way of life, indeed, which could save mankind from its mad rush towards self-annihilation—and that, therefore, it is the only goal worth striving for: while in their personal concerns and in their social behaviour, they drift further and further away from Islam. At no time in our modern history was there so much talk of Islam as in contemporary India; and at no time was there less effort on the part of Muslims to shape their individual lives and their communal affairs in accordance with the spirit of Islam.

Some of you will perhaps, at this juncture, be moved to protest against my assertion and will point to the great enthusiasm the Pakistan idea has created among the Muslims of this subcontinent. You will say—and rightly so—that the Muslims of India have at last awakened from their political torpor and have achieved a greater unanimity of purpose than ever before; that they have become fully conscious of having a separate cultural identity based on their being Muslims: that the foremost slogan of the Pakistan movement is *La ilaha ill Allah*; that they are imbued with the desire to establish political forms in which the Muslim worldview, Muslim ethics and Muslim social concepts could find their full expression; and you will ask me, in a somewhat aggrieved voice, whether I count all this for nothing from the Islamic point of view?

As a matter of fact, I do not "count all this for nothing"; I count it for very much indeed. I do believe (and have believed for about fourteen years) that there is no future for Islam in India until Pakistan becomes a reality; and that, if it becomes a reality here, it might bring about a spiritual revolution in the whole Muslim world by proving that it is possible to establish an *ideological* Islamic polity in our times no less than it was possible thirteen hundred years ago. But ask yourselves: are all leaders of the Pakistan movement and the intelligentsia which forms its spearhead quite serious in their avowals that Islam, and nothing but Islam, provides the ultimate inspiration of their struggle? Are they really aware of what it implies when they say, "The objective of Pakistan is *la ilaha ill'Allah*!" Do we all mean the same when we talk and dream of Pakistan?

These are big questions—so big that they stand out far above the present turmoil, far even above the individual sufferings which so many Muslim men and women in this country are now undergoing; for an answer to these questions will decide whether those sufferings herald a new vision of the future as a complete vindication of Islam as a "practical proposition"— or merely an improvement, by means of a national Muslim state, of our community's economic situation.

I hope the reader will forgive me if I quote myself. In the February 1947 number of *Arafat* (p. 166), I wrote:

> *"The Pakistan movement... can become the starting point of a new Islamic development if the Muslims realise—and continue realising it when Pakistan is achieved—that the real, historic justification of this movement does not consist in our dressing or talking or salaaming differently from the other inhabitants of*

the country, or in the grievances which we may have against other communities, or even in the desire to provide more economic opportunities and more elbow-room for people who—by sheer force of habit—call themselves 'Muslims'; but that such a justification is to be found only in the Muslims' desire to establish a truly Islamic polity; in other words, to translate the tenets of Islam into terms of practical life."

This, in short, is my conception of Pakistan; and I do not think that I am far wrong in assuming that it is the conception of many other Muslims as well. Of many, but not of all; and not even of most of them. For, by far, the larger parts of our intelligentsia do not seem to consider Pakistan in this light. To them, it means no more and no less than a way to freeing the Muslims of India from Hindu domination and the establishment of a political structure in which the Muslim community would find its "place in the sun" in the economic sense. Islam comes into the picture only in so far as it happens to be the religion of the people concerned—just as Catholicism came into the picture in the Irish struggle for independence because it happened to be the religion of most Irishmen. And just as Irish Catholicism was, in the last analysis, merely an additional feature— an emotional accompaniment, as it were—of Irish nationalism, so the Islamic slogans of the Pakistan movement are in danger of becoming, to many Muslims, merely an emotional accompaniment to their struggle for communal "self-determination".

To put it bluntly, many of our brothers and sisters do not seem to care for the spiritual, *Islamic* objectives of Pakistan and permit themselves to be carried away by sentiments not far removed from nationalism; and this is especially true of many Muslims educated on Western lines. Their indifference to Islam as a religion has grown considerably in the past decades; the duties which the *Shari'ah* imposes on many have mostly become irksome to them; they are unable to think otherwise than in Western patterns of thought, and so they do not believe in their hearts that the world's social and political problems are capable of being subordinated to purely religious considerations. Hence, their approach to Islam is governed by convention rather than ideology, and amounts, at best, to a faintly "cultural" interest in their community's "historical traditions". To such a mentality, the cry for Pakistan is just another national cry on the lines of "Egypt for the Egyptians" or "Czechoslovakia for the Czechoslovakians": namely, a demand for self-determination on the part of a group of people who have certain economic interests and certain cultural traits in common— one of those cultural traits being, in this case, our community's nominal adherence to Islam. Just that. No more, and no less.

Now this, you will admit, is a very poor view of Pakistan; a view, moreover, which does not do justice to the Islamic enthusiasm at present so markedly—if chaotically—displayed by the overwhelming masses of our common people. While many of our so-called intelligentsia are interested in Islam only in so far as it fits into their struggle for political self-determination, the common people most obviously desire self-determination for the sake of Islam as such; but, being inarticulate in their desire, and, as a rule, ignorant of the ways to its achievement, they naturally depend on the intelligentsia for leadership. The spiritual quality of that leadership will, ultimately, decide the quality of the Muslims' struggle for Pakistan— and the form which Pakistan itself will assume.

The Uniqueness of Pakistan

As far as the Muslim masses are concerned, the Pakistan movement is rooted in their instinctive feeling that they are an *ideological community* and have as such every right to an autonomous political existence. In other words, they feel and know that their communal existence is not—as with other communities—based on racial affinities or on the consciousness of cultural traditions held in common, but only—exclusively—on the fact of their common adherence to the ideology of Islam; and that, therefore, they must justify their communal existence by erecting a socio-political structure in which that ideology— the *Shari'ah*—would become the visible expression of their nationhood.

This, and not a solution of the all-India problem of Muslim minorities, is the real, historic purpose of the Pakistan movement. In so far as there will always remain non-Muslim minorities in Pakistan as well as Muslim minorities in the rest of India, Pakistan cannot be said to solve the minorities' problem in its entirety. But this is precisely a point which we—and our opponents—would do well to understand; the problem of minorities, however important in all considerations of India's political future, is, in itself, not fundamentally responsible for the Pakistan movement, but is rather an *incidental* accompaniment to the movement's intrinsic objective—the establishment of an Islamic polity in which our ideology could come to practical fruition. Only thus can we understand why the Muslims in, say, Bombay or Madras—who, of course, cannot expect that their provinces would become part of Pakistan—are as much interested in its realisation as are the Muslims of the Punjab or Bengal. They are interested in Pakistan not because they hope to come within its orbit in a territorial sense, but because they feel, as intensely as their brethren in the so-called "Muslim majority" provinces, that the birth of an Islamic polity in Pakistan would vindicate the claim that Islam is a practical proposition and that the Muslims— *because* of their being Muslims— are a nation unto themselves, irrespective of their geographical location. And if non-Muslims object to this claim on the grounds that nowhere else in the world— not even in the rest of the Muslim world—does any group of people nowadays aspire to separate nationhood by virtue of its religious beliefs alone, we are entitled to answer them: "In that case, we are unique. So what?"

So what? Should we concede to others the right to decide what should and what should not constitute our nationhood? Should we be ashamed of the fact that our political ideals are entirely different from the present-day ideals of the Turks, the Egyptians, the Afghans, the Syrians or the Iranians? Should we not, rather, derive pride from the thought that we alone among all the Muslim peoples are now finding the way back to the concept of the *ummah* enunciated by the Greatest Man?

For, in this respect, the Pakistan movement is truly unique among all the political mass movements now evident everywhere in the Muslim world.

No doubt, in the vast territories that go by this name, there are many other lovers of Islam besides us; in almost every Muslim country, there are selfless people who endeavour to propagate the Prophet's ﷺ teachings and to raise the moral level of the community; but nowhere in the modern world, except in the Pakistan movement, has a whole Muslim nation set out on the march towards Islam. No mass movement anywhere else in the Muslim world owes its origin to a similar Islamic inspiration on the part of the people; nor has any of the existing Muslim states a similar objective in view. Some of those states, like Turkey and Iran, are explicitly anti-Islamic in their governmental aims and openly declare that Islam should be eliminated from politics and from the people's social life. But even those Muslim states, in which religion is still being valued—in varying degrees—as a spiritual treasure, are "Islamic" only in so far as Islam is the religion professed by the majority inhabitants; while their political aims are not really governed by Islamic considerations but, rather, by what the rulers or ruling classes conceive as "national" interests in exactly the sense in which national interests are conceived in the West. It is, therefore, impossible to expect of such political organisations— whether they be autocratic kingdoms like Saudi Arabia or Afghanistan, republics like Syria, or constitutional monarchies like Egypt and Iraq—any clear impetus in the direction of Islam. This does not, of course, mean that all the people or even the rulers of those countries are indifferent to Islam as such; it means no more and no less than their attachment to Islam—genuine in many cases— has, for various historical reasons, no direct relation to the forms of their states and the aims of their government.

In the Pakistan movement, on the other hand, there undoubtedly exists a direct connection between the people's attachment to Islam and their political aims. Rather more than that; the practical success of this movement is exclusively due to our people's passionate, if as yet inarticulate, desire to have a state in which the forms and objectives of government would be determined by the *ideological* imperatives of Islam—a state, that is, in which Islam would not be just a religious and cultural "label" of the people concerned, but the very goal and purpose of state-formation. And it goes without saying that an achievement of such an Islamic state—the first in the modern world—would revolutionise Muslim political thought everywhere and would probably inspire other Muslim peoples to strive towards similar ends; and so it might become a prelude to an Islamic reorientation in many parts of the world.

It is, thus quite legitimate to say that the Pakistan movement contains a great promise for an Islamic revival; and, as far as I can see, it offers almost the only hope of such a revival in a world that is rapidly slipping away from the ideals of Islam. But the hope is justified only so long as our leaders, and the masses with them, keep the true objective of Pakistan in view and do not yield to the temptation to regard their movement as just another of the many "national" movements so fashionable in the present-day Muslim world—a danger which, I believe, is very imminent. I do not mean a nationalism based on racial lines, as we see it elsewhere (for such a tendency is impossible among Indian Muslims who, as a community, are composed of most diverse racial elements); but there is an acute danger of the Pakistan movement being deflected from its *ideological* course by laying too much stress on a "cultural" nationalism on a community of interests arising not so much from a common ideology as from the desire to preserve certain cultural traits, social habits and customs and, last but not least, to safeguard the economic development of a group of people who happen to be "Muslims" only by virtue of their birth. Nobody can doubt that the cultural traditions and the immediate economic requirements of the Muslim community are extremely important in our planning the Muslim future on Islamic lines. But this is just the point; they should never be viewed independently of our *ideological* goal: the building of our future on Islamic lines.

It appears, however, that the majority of our intelligentsia often convey the impression that the "actual" interests of the Muslim world could be viewed independently of what is described as the "purely *ideological*" interests of Islam;

in other words, that it is possible to be a good Pakistani without being *primarily* interested in Islam as the basic reality in one's own and in the community's life.

I hope that my readers will agree with me that such an arbitrary division between "Muslim" and "Islamic" interests is sheer nonsense. Islam is not just one among several characteristics of Muslim communal existence but its only historical cause and justification; and to consider Muslim interests as something apart from Islam is like considering a living being as something apart from the fact of its life. But however nonsensical such an attitude may appear to a thinking person, there is no going round the fact that most people (not excluding most of our intelligentsia) are in the habit of never thinking at all...

Evasion and Self-Deception

How many, of our leaders, and of our intelligentsia in general, have an *Islamic* polity in view when they appeal to the Muslims to close their ranks and to sacrifice their all, if necessary, for the achievement of Pakistan? Is it not, rather, true that, as a rule, they are far more concerned with the movement's negative aspect—the impossibility, for the Muslims, to attain to a "place in the sun" under non-Muslim domination—than with its positive aspect—our desire to build our socio-political existence in terms of Islam and for the sake of Islam? Is it not true that to many educated Muslims, and to some of our leaders as well, Islam means no more than a tactical weapon in their community's struggle with non-Muslims, not a goal for its own sake, but an argument, not a genuine hope, but a slogan? Is it, in short, not true that many of our protagonists are far more concerned with obtaining more political power and more economic amenities for a nominally Muslim community than with converting that nominally Muslim community into an *Islamic* community?'

> *"I do not wish to belittle what our leaders have done for us. In some respects, their achievement is great and deserves the highest praise."*

They have succeeded in rousing the dormant strength of the community and in bringing about a sense of unity never before witnessed in the modern Muslim world. This much every sensible person will readily admit. But what I blame some of our leaders for is their apparent inability to rise to the spiritual greatness displayed by the Muslim masses in this decisive hour of their destiny and to deliberately guide the ideal which is fundamentally responsible for their present upheaval. To put it into simple words: our leaders do not seem to make a serious attempt to show that Islam is the paramount objective of their struggle. They do, no doubt, talk about Islam whenever they issue a statement or address a public gathering—but their references to it are always in the future tense, and hardly ever an attempt is made to bring the community's present mode of life and thought into greater agreement with the principles of Islam. This, I believe, is a very great omission. We should not forget that the future is, invariably, a child of the present; that is to say, the manner of our life today is bound to influence the quality of our tomorrow. If the meaning of our struggle for Pakistan is truly to be found in the words *la ilaha ill'Allah*, our present behaviour must be come nearer and nearer to this ideal—that is, of becoming better Muslims not only in our words, but in our actions as well.

It should be our leaders' duty to tell their followers that they must become better Muslims *today* in order to be worthy of Pakistan *tomorrow*; instead of which they merely assure us that we shall become better Muslims "as soon as Pakistan is achieved."

This easy assurance will not do. It is self-deceptive in the extreme. If we do not sow the seeds of Islamic life now, when our enthusiasm is at its fighting pitch, there is no earthly reason to expect that we will suddenly be transformed into better Muslims when the struggle is over and our political autonomy secured.

I can almost hear some of our leaders say: Brother, you are pessimistic—or perhaps a little bit too apprehensive. Almost every one of us desires a truly Islamic life. Only, it would be impolitic to insist on this ideal right now. In our ranks, there are many people who render the most valuable services to our political cause, but— owing to wrong upbringing—do not care too much for religion; and if we stress the religious side of our struggle from the very beginning, those valuable workers might cool down in their zeal and so be lost to our cause. We do not want to lose Them; we cannot afford to lose them and so we are obliged to postpone our work for the people's religious upliftment until after we have won a state of our own. At present, we must concentrate all our energies on the short-term objective before us—the freeing of the Muslims from non-Muslim domination—and not dissipate them on purely religious considerations. If we insist, at this stage, too loudly on our long-term objective—the deepening of Islamic consciousness in the Muslims and the creation of a truly Islamic polity—we might not only estrange many of our Westernised brothers and sisters from our cause, but also increase the apprehensions of the non-Muslim minorities who live in the area of Pakistan."

Now, I personally believe that the above reasoning is extremely fallacious and intellectually dishonest. Let us consider the two points mentioned therein one by one, beginning with the second.

As for the apprehensions, which our insistence on an Islamic life might cause among the non-Muslim minorities, I should like you to ask yourselves: What is it that makes non-Muslims so bitterly antagonistic to the idea of Pakistan? Obviously, a fear of what they describe as a "communal *raj*' and the probability of the Muslim-dominated areas being cut off from the rest of India. The question as to whether the Muslims *truly* intend to live according to the principles of Islam or not leaves the non-Muslims cold. They are afraid of Muslims; political preponderance in certain areas and it does not make *prima facie* the least difference to them whether the Muslims are inspired in their endeavours by Islamic or any other considerations. Hence, they will oppose Muslim endeavours in any case and with all the strength at their disposal.

With all this, the attitude of our opponents might—though I do not say that it definitely will—be to some extent influenced by the thought that what we Muslims really aim at is *justice for all*; provided that we succeed in convincing them that we are really moved by moral convictions and not by a wish to exploit non-Muslims for the benefit of Muslims. It is, therefore, our duty to prove to the whole world that we really mean to live up to the standard laid down in these words of the Holy Qur'an:

كُنتُمْ خَيرُ اُمَّةٍ اُخرِجَتْ لِلنَّاسِ تَأمُرُوْنَ بِالْمَعْرُوْفِ وَتَنْهَوْنَ عَنِ الْمُنْكَرِ وَتُؤْمِنُوْنَ بِاللهِ

"You are the best community that has been sent forth unto mankind: for you enjoin the Right and forbid the Wrong, and have faith in God"
(Al-Imran 3:110).

Our being a worthy ummah in the sight of God depends on our being prepared to struggle, always and under all circumstances, for the upholding of justice and the abolition of injustice; and this should preclude the possibility of a truly Islamic community being unjust to non-Muslims. I can well imagine that a non-Muslim feels apprehensive about his future in a state which, in his opinion, would aim at giving economic preference to the Muslim community at the expense of non-Muslims, but he will have less reason to feel such an apprehension if he becomes convinced that the Muslims are determined to ensure justice to Muslims and non-Muslims alike. And we cannot convince our opponents of our bona fides unless we prove, firstly, that an Islamic polity connotes justice for all, and, secondly, that we

Muslims are really serious in our avowals that precisely such, a polity is our goal—in other words, that we truly believe in the tenets of our religion. It is, therefore, quite erroneous to assume that the fears of non-Muslim minorities could be allayed by our discreetly avoiding, as much as possible, any direct references to our ultimate religious objectives. This only creates in them a suspicion of hypocrisy on our part. The real way to allaying or at least alleviating their fears would be our clear exposition, in as great detail as possible, of the ethical ideals towards which we are striving; but even such an exposition will be of no avail unless we are able to show, in our day-to-day life, that those ideals mean more to us than mere slogans.

Apart from its probable effect on non-Muslims, an evasive postponement of our "long-term", Islamic objectives in favour of what some people regard (quite wrongly) as momentarily "expedient" or "political" must have a detrimental effect on our community's moral tenor and can only result in our greater estrangement from the ways of true Islam. Instead of becoming increasingly aware of the ideal goal before them, the Muslims will again become accustomed to think—as they did for many centuries—in terms of "expediency" and immediate convenience, and the Islamic objective of Pakistan will most definitely recede into the realm of theoretical idealism— in exactly the same manner as the true objectives of Christianity have receded among the so-called Christian nations of the West.

We do not want that. We want, through Pakistan, to make Islam a *reality* in our lives. We want Pakistan in order that every one of us should be able to live a truly Islamic life in the widest sense of the word. And it is admittedly impossible for an individual to live in accordance with the scheme propounded by God's Apostle unless the whole society consciously conforms to it and makes the law of Islam the law of the land.

But this kind of Pakistan will never materialise unless we postulate the law of Islam not merely as an ideal for a vaguely defined future but as the basis, wherever possible, of all our social and personal behaviour at this very hour and minute. That there are, in our midst, many people to whom religion is unimportant to such an extent that they might "take offence" at our insisting on the religious side of our struggle should not carry the least weight in our considerations. The gentlemen and ladies of this kind will quickly enough subordinate themselves to the will of the community if they are made to realise that the community as a whole is determined to march towards Islam. In any case, their individual preferences must not be allowed to affect our determination. Can you imagine that the Holy Prophet ﷺ would ever have consented to postpone, even for a single day, his insistent demand for a fulfilment of the "long- term" ideals of Islam in order to avoid "giving offence" to the idolatrous Quraysh, so that they might help him in building a Muslim state?

"Well," you might say, "the Prophet was a prophet, and so he could afford to be uncompromising. But we are ordinary people" To which I would answer: do you believe in the injunction:

لَقَدْ كَانَ لَكُمْ فِيْ رَسُوْلِ اللهِ أُسْوَةٌ حَسَنَةٌ

'Verily, in the Apostle of God you have the best example' (al-Ahzab 33:21)?

Don't you think that this injunction refers to your politics as much as to your prayers; to your public life as much as to your personal concerns?

The Choice Before Us

It is a sign of our spiritual confusion—due to the long centuries of our decadence—that the one political movement which holds the promise of an Islamic revival at the same time threatens to defeat its innermost purpose and to degenerate into something very much akin to the "national" movements of, say, Egypt, Turkey or Syria. There is a definite, though perhaps involuntary, tendency on the part of many of our leaders to ignore the spiritual, Islamic background of our struggle and to justify the Muslims' demand for freedom by stressing their unfortunate experiences with the Hindu majority as well as to base the Muslims' claim to being a separate nation on the differences between their and the Hindus' social usages and cultural expressions. In short, there is a mounting inclination to consider the fact—for a fact it—of a separate Muslim nationhood in the conventional Western sense of the word "nation" instead of considering it in the Islamic sense of *Ummah* or *millat*. Why should we hesitate to proclaim, loudly and without fear, that our being a nation has nothing to do with the conventional meaning of this word; That we are a nation not merely because our habits, customs, and cultural expressions are different from those of the other groups inhabiting the country, but *because we mean to shape our life in accordance with a particular ideal of our own?*

It cannot be often enough repeated that our adherence to the teachings of Islam is the only justification of our communal existence. We are not a racial entity. We are—in spite of the great progress of Urdu as the language of Muslim India—not even a linguistic entity within the strict meaning of this term. We are not, and never can be, a nation in the sense in which the English or the Arabs or the

Chinese are nations. But precisely the fact that we are not, and never can be, a nation in the exclusive conventional sense of the word is the innermost source of our strength, for it makes us realise that we—we alone in the modern world—can, if we but want it, bring again to life that glorious vision which arose over the sands of Arabia nearly fourteen centuries ago: the vision of an *ummah* of free men and women bound together not by the accidental bonds of race and birth but by their free, conscious allegiance to a common ideal.

Unfortunately, some of the most active of our leaders belong to that disillusioned, sceptical class of Muslims to whom Islam is nothing but a "cultural tradition" and to whom, consequently, Pakistan means no more than the first step on the road which the so-called "advanced" Muslim nations are treading—namely, the road to full-fledged nationalism. In spite of their frequent, verbose insistence on the Islamic aspect of our struggle, this kind of leader thinks it more "modern" to avoid any allusion to the necessity for Muslims of shaping their lives here and now in accordance with the religious principles of Islam—to the necessity, that is, of identifying their demand for Pakistan with a serious desire for a fulfilment of Islam's ideals in the personal and social concerns of their lives. It goes without saying that such a half-hearted attitude deprives the idea of Pakistan of its most dynamic—because spiritual—purport and this is a far greater threat to its future than any opposition from outside could ever be.

For the destiny of great nations and communities does not, in the last resort, depend on whether their neighbours *a priori* agree with their aims or oppose them: it depends, invariably and irrevocably, on the spiritual strength—or weakness—of those responsible for those aims. If our desire for Pakistan is an outcome of our creative strength and purity; if we attain to that clarity of vision which encompasses the goal of our endeavours long before it is achieved; if we learn to love that goal for its own sake—in the conviction that it is supremely good in an absolute sense (or, as I would prefer to phrase it, in God's sight) and not merely because it appears to be economically advantageous to ourselves and our community, then no power on earth could stop Pakistan from being born and from becoming a gateway to an Islamic revival all over the world. And if, on the other hand, our cry for self-determination is due to no more than a fear of being dominated by a non-Muslim majority; if our vision of the future is merely negative; if it does not encompass the hope of our being free for something but contents itself with the beggarly hope of our being free from something; if Islam, instead of being a moral obligation and an end in itself, means no more to us than a habit and a cultural label, then—even then—we might achieve some sort of Pakistan by virtue of our numerical strength in this country; but it would be an achievement far short of the tremendous possibilities which God seems to be offering to us. It would be only one "national state" more in a world split up into numberless national states—perhaps no worse than some of the others, but certainly no better than most; while the subconscious dream of the Muslim masses, and the conscious dream of those who first spoke of Pakistan (long before even this name had been thought of) was the birth of a polity in which the Prophet's ﷺ Message could fully come into its own as a practical proposition.

The Time for a Decision

If our present leaders listen to the people's heartbeat, they are bound to realise that what the common man desires is not merely a state in which Muslims would have greater economic facilities than they have now but a state in which God's Word would reign supreme. Not that the "common man" does not care for economic facilities. He cares, rightly, very much for them. But he feels, no less rightly, that an Islamic theocracy would not only give him all the economic justice and opportunity for material development which he now so sadly lacks but would enhance his human dignity and spiritual security as well.

This feeling, this expectation of our common people is, as I have already mentioned, largely inchoate and confused. It is instinctive rather than intellectual. They cannot yet clearly visualise the shape which that theocracy should have, nor are they fully aware of the effort it will cost to achieve it. How could it be otherwise? For centuries, they have been estranged from the genuine teachings of Islam; from time immemorial, they have been steeped in ignorance, superstition, political humiliation; is it a wonder, then, that they rely only on catchwords and slogans and are unable to give, all at once, a coherent, valid expression to their innermost dreams and desires? That they are unable to find, all at once, their bearings in the volcanic upheaval into which those dreams and desires have thrown them? That, in a word, they need spiritual leadership no less than leadership in the field of political tactics?

To give valid Islamic content, as well as a creative, positive direction to the people's dreams and desires; to prepare them not only politically (in the conventional context of this word) but also spiritually and *ideologically* for the great goal of Pakistan, this is the supreme task awaiting our leaders. They must not think that to organise the masses and to give voice to our political demands is all that the *millat* expects them to do. Organisation is, no doubt, urgently necessary; political agitation is necessary, but these necessities must be made to serve our *ideological* goal—and not, as we so often find it in these days, allowed to be reduced to secondary rank. To a Muslim who takes Islam seriously, every political endeavour must, in the last resort, derive its sanction from religion, just as religion can never remain aloof from politics for the simple reason that Islam, being concerned not only with our spiritual development but with the manner of our physical, social and economic existence as well, is a "political" creed in the deepest, most morally compelling sense of this term. In other words, the Islamic, religious aspect of our fight for Pakistan must be made predominant in all the appeals which Muslim leaders make to the Muslim masses. If this demand is neglected, our struggle cannot possibly fulfil its historic mission.

1 - These principles have been set out by me in the July 1947 number of *Arafat* in an essay entitled "Towards an Islamic Constitution".

The need for *ideological,* Islamic leadership on the part of our leaders is the paramount need of the day. That some of them— though by far not all—are really aware of their great responsibility in this respect is evident, for example, from the splendid Convocation Address which Liaquat Ali Khan, the *Quaid-i-Azam*'s principal lieutenant, delivered at Aligarh a few months ago. In that address he vividly stressed the fact that our movement derives its ultimate inspiration from the Holy Qur'an, and that, therefore, the Islamic state at which we are aiming should derive its authority from the *Shari'ah* alone. Muhammad Ali Jinnah himself has spoken in a similar vein on many occasions. Such pronouncements, coming as they do from the highest levels of the Muslim League leadership, go a long way to clarifying the League's aims. But a clarification of aims is not enough. If these ideal aims are to have a practical effect on our politics, the High Command of the League should insist on a more concrete elaboration by a competent body of our intellectual leaders, of the principles on which Pakistan shall be built.

This was perhaps not so very urgent a few years back when our political goal was no more than a distant ideal. But, as it happens, the tremendous changes with which this country has now faced have made the achievement of Pakistan a very real probability for our immediate future. More than that, it is virtually certain that we shall have a Pakistan state in some form or other before June 1948. But this is just the point we must bear in mind: there will be a Pakistan "in some form or other" and it is for us to decide what form it shall have. You must, therefore, admit that the question, "Do we really want Islam?" has been lifted from the realm of mere pious contemplation and has at last become a question of immediate, practical politics.

It is quite possible that before these lines appear in print, the *Quaid-i-Azam* will have sent forth a call to the Muslim nation to establish a Constituent Assembly for Pakistan; or, if this has not been done so far, it is bound to be done in the very near future. Hence, Muslim legislators and intellectuals must make up their minds here and now as to what sort of political structure, what sort of society, and what sort of national ideals they are going to postulate.

The fundamental issue before them is simple enough: shall our state be just another symbol of the worldwide flight from religion, just one more of the many "Muslim" states in which Islam has no influence whatsoever on the community's social and political behaviour, or shall it become the most exciting, most glorious experiment in modern history, our first step on the road which the Greatest Man has pointed out to mankind? Shall Pakistan be only a means of "national" development of Muslims in certain areas of India or shall it herald, all over the world, the majestic rebirth of Islam as a practical, political proposition?

If ever there was a time in which a community was called upon to make a conscious decision about its future, this time has come for us now. And it is for our leaders to exercise that decision.

Never before have Muslim leaders been endowed with such power to guide the destinies of the *millat* in the right direction, or in the wrong. It is within their power to decide, here and now, whether Indian Muslims shall become Muslims in the true sense of the word, and thus, the core and backbone of a resurgent Islam, or just another "national group" among many other so-called Muslim groups and states where Islam is good enough to be displayed as a cultural label but not good enough to provide the basis on which to build the community's social, economic and political existence. The present leaders of the Muslim League, I repeat it deliberately, have it within their power to make such a decision, for the wave of enthusiasm for Pakistan which has swept over the Muslim masses in this country, and which has united them as they have never been united in the past, has endowed those leaders with a prestige—and a power to lead—the like of which was never enjoyed by leaders in past centuries. Because of this, their moral responsibility is all the greater. They must not think that it begins and ends with political "manoeuvring" or "tactics", for, however necessary such purely tactical moves may be, they represent only a side issue, a passing phase of the leaders' duties—their main duty being that of nation-building. And as the basis of our nationhood is Islam, all of our leaders should begin to think in terms of Islam right now, instead of deferring such a reorientation of thought to a future time ("we shall see to these matters after Pakistan has been achieved"); and they must not permit themselves to draw—as many of them seem to be inclined to do—a fanciful dividing line between the demands of Islam and the "temporary" interests of the Muslim community, for, in truth, nothing could be more conducive to the best interests of the community—in political no less than in spiritual concerns—than its complete, conscious surrender to the demands of Islam.

In short, it is the foremost duty of our political leaders to impress upon the masses that the objective of Pakistan is the establishment of a truly Islamic polity and that this objective can never be attained unless every fighter for Pakistan—man or woman, great or small—honestly tries to come closer to Islam at every hour and every minute of his or her life; that, in a word, only a good Muslim can be a good Pakistani.

Our Moral Stature

And this holds good for the leaders themselves as well. They must show, in their social behaviour, that they regard Islam as a serious proposition and not merely as a slogan; to put it plainly, that they themselves are trying to live up to the demands of Islam. I do not mean to say that all of them are remiss in this respect. There are among them many people to whom Islam is a living inspiration, and to these our homage is due. But, on the other hand, very many of our leaders have Islam only on their lips—and that only when they address a public meeting or make a statement to the press—while their personal behaviour and outlook is as devoid of Islam as the behaviour and outlook of the average political leader in Europe or America is devoid of Christianity. This must change if our struggle for Pakistan is not to degenerate into a pitiful copy of the "nationalist" endeavours from which the rest of the Muslim world is suffering. Though it may not be our business to sit in judgment over a person's beliefs—this being God's business alone—the *millat* does have the right to expect of its leaders that their way of life conforms to the ideology which they profess to defend.

But even if our leaders do attain to the most sublime heights of Islamic consciousness, their example alone will not suffice to safeguard our spiritual goal. Our community as a whole must be lifted up from the abyss of the moral and social decay in which it now finds itself. Our present moral stature is far below what is demanded of us by Islam. We lack civic spirit; we love the easy life; we do not mind telling lies whenever we think them advantageous to our supposed self-interest; we break our promises; we smile indulgently upon the most barefaced corruption, selfishness and trickery in our business affairs; most of us are mainly concerned with what is described as a "career" and with obtaining petty advantages for ourselves and our relatives; we are always ready to malign other Muslims behind their backs; in short, we do not seem to have derived the least benefit from the very fount of our existence: the teachings of Islam. And how can we hope to be worthy of a truly Islamic Pakistan? How can we hope to achieve such a Pakistan if we do not make the least attempt to rise from our moral depths? How can we hope to arrive at an equitable social order as long as the only source of all true equity—the love and fear of God—is absent from our hearts? There is, I am sure, no answer to these questions. Unless the Muslims radically improve their ways and moral standards and cease to flout the ordinances of the Shari'ah at almost every step they make, the idea of Pakistan is bound to lose its spiritual purport and, thus, its unique position in the modern history of Islam.

As I have already said, the Muslim masses instinctively realise the Islamic purport of Pakistan and genuinely desire a state of affairs in which *La ilaha illA'llah* would become the starting point of the community's development. But they are inarticulate and confused in their thoughts. They cannot find their way unaided. They must be led. And so, again, we come back to the question of leadership and of its duties.

It seems to me that the supreme test of the present-day Muslim leadership will be its ability—or inability—to lead the community not only in the purely political and economic but also in the moral sphere; the ability—or inability—to convince the Muslims that:

إِنَّ اللّٰهَ لَا يُغَيِّرُ مَا بِقَوْمٍ حَتّٰى يُغَيِّرُوْا مَا بِاَنْفُسِهِمْ

"God does not change the condition of a people unless they change their inner selves" (Al-Ra'd 13:11)

which means no more and no less than that a community's political and economic status cannot be lastingly improved unless the community as a whole grows in moral stature.*

*(*Arafat* (Lahore), (May 1947) pp. 231-254

Appendix V

TOWARDS AN ISLAMIC CONSTITUTION

قُلِ اللّٰهُمَّ مٰلِكَ الْمُلْكِ تُؤْتِي الْمُلْكَ مَنْ تَشَآءُ وَتَنْزِعُ الْمُلْكَ مِمَّنْ تَشَآءُ ۔ وَتُعِزُّ مَنْ تَشَآءُ وَتُذِلُّ
مَنْ تَشَآءُ ۚ بِيَدِكَ الْخَيْرُ ۚ اِنَّكَ عَلٰى كُلِّ شَيْءٍ قَدِيرٌ

"Say: O God, Lord of Sovereignty! Thou givest sovereignty to whom Thou pleasest, and takest away sovereignty from whom Thou pleasest. Thou exaltest whom Thou pleasest, and abasest whom Thou pleasest. In Thy hand is all good. Lo! Thou hast power over all things." (Al-Imran 3: 26)

Secular or Islamic?

In every nation's life there comes, sooner or later, a moment when it seems to be given a free choice of its destiny, a moment when the decision as to what way to take, what future to aim at, seems to be freed from all that outside pressure which "circumstances" usually impose on us and when no power on earth is able to prevent us from choosing one way in preference to another. These moments are extremely rare and fleeting and it may well be that if a nation fails to avail itself of the opportunity thus offered, it may not be offered another for centuries to come.

Such a moment of free choice has now arrived for the Muslim nation of Pakistan. After a decade of struggle, hope, disappointment and partial achievements independence has been won; and now it is for the nation to decide what to do with that independence. It is for the nation to decide, without let or hindrance, whether

Pakistan shall be an Islamic state in the true sense of the word—an entirely new beginning for ourselves as well as for the whole Muslim world—or just another "national" state in which Islam will be subordinated to other interests. There is no gainsaying that countless Muslims desire from their hearts the first of these two alternatives; but there is, also, no doubt that very strong forces are at work to deflect the masses from their Islamic goal and to make Pakistan a "secular" state in deference to what the majority of mankind today regards as desirable. For the majority of people in almost all countries have grown accustomed to look upon institutional religion as something antiquated, and therefore not quite "respectable" from the intellectual point of view; as something out of tune with modern endeavours—supposed to be an evidence of "progressive mentality"—to free man from all moral obligations not devised by himself; as something, in short, that enlightened people cannot be expected to consider seriously in the context of national, social and economic planning; and, for this reason, a suggestion to build a state on the basis of religion is usually described as "reactionary" or, at the best—with smiling condescension—as "impractical idealism."

But the ironic beauty of the thing lies in the fact that a genuinely Islamic state is far more "practical"—that is, far easier to establish and far more likely to lead to the nation's social and economic success—than any state in which religion is relegated to the second rank or disregarded entirely. Why such a "theocratic" state is easier to establish will be shown in this and the subsequent issues of *Arafat*, and why it is more likely to result in greater public welfare and happiness will, I hope, become obvious from what I am just going to say.

A theocratic state must be, *prima facie*, an *ideological* organisation. As such it cannot content itself, like a "national" state, with simply safeguarding the cultural and economic interests of a particular group of people inhabiting a particular geographical space but must also endeavour to direct the community under its jurisdiction towards the attainment of definite, *ideological* ends. Whatever its ends, an *ideological* state is not just a utilitarian organisation devised for the benefit of a particular closed society (the "nation") but, on the contrary, presupposes the existence of an open society—a community of ideas open to all people regardless of their geographical or racial origin. Hence, while a "national" state need not, and does not, look to anything but the variable interests of an already existing group and always acts on the principle "right or wrong, my country" (or, "my nation"), an *ideological* state presumes the existence of an invariable, moral obligation arising from a universal law, which means that the state derives its sanction from, and exists for the sake of, the people's acceptance of that law. Now this, in its turn, presupposes— especially in the case of a religious state—a more or less general acceptance by the people of a particular, definite outlook on life and a definite scale of moral values by which to judge between right and wrong in the nation's affairs; that is to say, it presupposes that "right" and "wrong" have an ethical *permanency* corresponding to a universal law. It is not difficult to realise that such a concept makes a theocratic state (which, in its very nature, is an *ideological* state par excellence) far more stable and cohesive than a "national "or "secular "state could ever be.

For in a "secular" state, there is no stable norm by which to discriminate between right and wrong. The only possible criterion is "the nation's interest." But it is obvious that, in the absence of an objective scale of moral values, different groups of people have widely divergent views as to what constitutes the nation's best interests. While a capitalist may believe (often quite sincerely) that civilisation must perish as soon as economic liberalism is superseded by socialism, a socialist may be (and frequently is) of the opinion that the very maintenance of civilisation depends on the abolition of capitalism; and both make their moral views dependent on their economic views. I am giving this only as an example; in reality, the existing ethical differences within, and between, "secular" societies are innumerable and very far-reaching. This is unavoidable as long as the discrimination between right and wrong, between what should and what should not be done, is left to the mercy of individual or group interests—in other words, to people's changing preferences. If we admit that this is a natural (and therefore desirable) state of mankind's affairs, we admit, by implication, that the terms "right" and "wrong" have no permanent meaning in themselves but are conditioned by interests, time and circumstances. In logical pursuit of this thought, we have no choice but to deny the existence of any moral obligation as such—for moral obligation is meaningless if it is not conceived as something absolute. As soon as we begin to believe that our concepts of right and wrong, or good and evil, are mere products of convention and environment, and therefore variable, they cannot serve us as guides in determining the course which our affairs should take; and so, in planning our affairs, we can be guided by expediency alone. Now "expediency" is an extremely elastic term. What is expedient to you need not be (and usually is not) expedient to me—with the result that our interests must, at some point, come to a clash; and the more we struggle against another, the wider our interests diverge and the more antagonistic become our ideas as to what is right and what wrong.

This is, in short, what is happening in the world today. I do not refer primarily to the international conflicts which have become so permanent a fixture in our time (though these also are a result of conflicting views as to what is "expedient"); I refer, mainly, to the spectacle of inner dissension, a characteristic of almost all modern states and nations. No nation or community can remain really united unless it has, or achieves, a certain degree of unanimity as to what is right and what is wrong; and no such unanimity is possible unless the nation or community agrees on a moral obligation anchored in a permanent, absolute, moral law. And it is only religion that can provide the basis for such an agreement. It does not, therefore, call for special cleverness to realise that a religious state offers an infinitely greater possibility of national happiness than any "secular" political organisation could offer, provided, of course, that the religious doctrine on which such a state rests—and from which it derives its sovereignty—makes full allowance for man's evolution by avoiding all rigidity in its concept of the law. And this is precisely what we claim for the religious doctrine summarised in the word Islam.

Why Islamic law?

As to the central concept underlying Islam's outlook on life, there can be no doubt at all in the mind of anyone who is acquainted, however superficially, with the Qur'an. In countless verses, the Holy Book makes it clear that the ultimate purpose of all creation is the compliance of the created with the Creator's Will. In the case of man, this compliance—called Islam—is postulated as a conscious, active coordination of man's desires and behaviour with the rules of life laid down by the Creator. Now this demand presupposes that—with reference to human life—the terms "good" and "evil" have a sharply circumscribed meaning, a meaning that does not change from case to case or from time to time but retains its validity for all times and conditions. Obviously, no definition of good and evil arrived at through our speculation can ever possess such eternal validity, for all human thought is essentially subjective and, therefore, strongly influenced by the thinker's time and environment. Hence, if it is really the purpose of religion to show man the way towards a coordination of his desires and his behaviour with the Creator's Will, he must be given a divine law which would teach him in unmistakable terms how to differentiate between good and evil and, consequently, what to do and what not to do. A mere general instruction in ethics—like "love your neighbour", "be truthful", "rely on God"—is not sufficient, because it is liable to most conflicting interpretations. What is needed is precise legislation which would outline, however broadly, the whole sphere of human life, in all its aspects: spiritual, physical, individual, social, economic and political.

Islam fills this want by means of a divine law—called *shari'ah*, which has been provided in the ordinances of the Qur'an and supplemented (or rather, detailed and exemplified) by the Prophet ﷺ in the course of his blessed life. It is the Qur'an itself which makes this double provision:

وَمَآ اٰتٰىكُمُ الرَّسُوْلُ فَخُذُوْهُ وَمَا نَهٰىكُمْ عَنْهُ فَانْتَهُوْا

"Whatever the Apostle commands you, accept, and whatever he forbids you, avoid" (al-Hashr 59: 7). And —

مَنْ يُّطِعِ الرَّسُوْلَ فَقَدْ اَطَاعَ اللّٰهَ

"Whoso obeys the Apostle, obeys God" (al-Nisa 4: 80).

Thus, whenever an Apostolic ordinance is authentically established as such, it has full *shar'iah* weight: and it is therefore legitimate to speak of the two sources of Islam—namely, Qur'an and Sunnah.

From the viewpoint of the believer, the two sources reveal to us a visible, conceptually understandable segment of God's all-embracing plan of creation. With reference to man and the "how" of man's behaviour on earth, they are the only available, positive statement (bayyinah) of what God wants us to do and to be. We may, of course, obtain further glimpses of what we describe as God's plan through observing and studying nature (an activity strongly recommended in the Qur'an); but, even if correct, the findings thus obtained will tell us only something about certain facts of nature, including ourselves, and about the inter-relation of those facts—but will never tell us directly how we human beings should behave. In other words, natural sciences aim only at discovering how things are, or, at most, how they might be or react under given circumstances. It is only indirectly, through speculative reasoning on the basis of certain sets of established facts, that science can attempt to advise us on what should be the course of our action in individual and social matters. But because science is always in a state of flux—subject to the unceasing discovery of "new" facts and, consequently, to an unceasing reinterpretation and revaluation of previously ascertained sets of facts—its advice is hesitant, spasmodic, and, at times, quite contradictory to previously tendered advice, which, in a nutshell, amounts to saying that science is never in a position to lay down, with absolute certainty and once and for all, what man should do or leave undone in order to achieve wellbeing and happiness. And, for this reason, science cannot (nor does it really attempt to) define "good" and "evil" in absolute terms and forever.

As already mentioned, the *shari'ah* undertakes just the thing which science is unable to undertake—namely, to provide man with practical directives of behaviour in absolute terms and for all circumstances. Because it is not a human but a divine law, it obviously cannot be, and actually never is, in conflict with any true finding of science. More than that: it does not depend for its validity on scientific discoveries and ever-changing interpretations of the facts of nature— for it has been conceived by Him to whom all nature owes its origin and existence. As long as we believe this, we must consider the *shari'ah* as the only positive indication of what God wishes us to do and to leave undone.

But He only indicates to us how He wishes us to behave. He does not physically compel us to behave in the way indicated. He gives us freedom of choice. We may, if we so desire, willingly submit to His revealed law and thus, as it were cooperate with Him; and we may, if we think it worthwhile, go against Him, disregard His law, and risk the consequences. However we decide, the responsibility is ours. It goes without saying that Islamic life depends on our making the former choice. Nevertheless, even if we choose to obey God, we may not always be able to do it fully, for a good deal of the divine law is concerned with communal matters—and so, it is obvious that, in the context of communal life, the rebellious behaviour of one person may make it difficult for other persons to live in accordance with Islam; and the larger the number of such "rebels," the greater the difficulty for the rest. In other words, none of us can ever lead an Islamic life in the fullest sense of the word unless the community as a whole is prepared to cooperate to that end. But even if the community as a whole is prepared to cooperate on Islamic lines, the cooperation must remain largely theoretical so long as there is no worldly power to enforce the law and to prevent rebellious behaviour—at least in matters of social concern—on the part of any of the community's members. Only the state can provide such power in an organised manner, and so the creation of an Islamic state is an indispensable condition of Islamic life.

Facing our Responsibility

There was a time when a discussion of the principles of the Islamic state had no more than academic flavour; for, even if we had desired it, there was no immediate possibility of our achieving an Islamic state. Now, however, we have such a possibility before us; and it is for us to convert the possibility into a certainty—or alternatively, to push it back again (God alone knows for how long) into the realm of academic speculations. There is no earthly power to prevent us from taking either of these two courses. However we choose, the responsibility will be ours, and ours alone.

In the preceding, I have referred to the sceptical attitude of many Muslims, and particularly educated Muslims, towards the desirability and practicability of a theocratic Islamic state. In this, as in so many other aspects of our contemporary life, the influence of Western thought is unmistakable. For reasons of its own, the West has become disappointed with religion, and this disappointment is reflected in the ethical and social chaos now pervading the major portion of the globe. Instead of submitting their decisions and actions to the criterion of a universal moral law— which is what religion ultimately aims at—the peoples of the West (and with them, their imitators in the East) have come to regard "expediency" as the only obligation to which men's affairs should be subjected; and because the ideas as to what is expedient naturally differ in every group, nation and community, the most bewildering conflicts of interests have come to the fore. None of the modern Western ideologies—communism, social democracy, economic liberalism, fascism, and so forth—are really able to transform that chaos into order; none of them make a serious attempt to consider economic or social problems under the aspect of unchangeable moral principles, and therefore, none of them have recommended itself to general acceptance. Even in countries in which there is a semblance of such "general" acceptance—as in the case of communism in Soviet Russia—unanimity is enforced from above with all the paraphernalia of dictatorship, secret police and social terror; and the very existence of such an apparatus of oppression shows that, in reality, there is no unanimous, popular acceptance at all. Communists will of course say that, in their case, oppressive dictatorship is "expedient" in view of the peculiar situation in Russia and in the world as a whole. But this is just the point: on the plea of "expediency", you may excuse anything; you may commit the most atrocious crimes and still have a smug feeling of self-righteousness. As a matter of fact, the crimes which Western civilisation—whether communist or capitalist—now inflicts on humanity (including itself) are being committed on this most convenient plea. And so long as this plea is maintained and naively regarded as valid by the masses of people, there can be no moral significance in the concept of the state.

We should think of this when we make our choice.

If we Muslims continue submitting our political, social and economic ideas to the ideas prevalent in the West, we are bound to join sooner or later (and probably very soon) its tragic dance towards chaos and self-destruction. We have nothing to gain and everything to lose by imitating Western concepts.

But we have, on the other hand, a lot to gain by endowing our state with a moral reality of its own, that is to say, by making it correspond to the ethical principles of Islam.

Even if the ethical outlook of the West did not—as, in fact, it does— contradict the outlook of Islam in almost every point, Islam's claim to be a self-contained code of life should be, for a Muslim, incentive enough to make this attempt. For if Islam is really a self-contained code of life, it must not only be able to direct man's spiritual endeavours but must be also in a position to tell him how to organise his society and how to build a state. And it must do this not merely by stating ethical principles in a general way (as, for instance, Christianity does) but by outlining a definite, concrete scheme; though, at the same time, the scheme must be sufficiently wide and elastic to permit its successful functioning at all stages of human development; In other words, it must be stated in a broad—though none the less definite—outline, leaving it to the human *ijtihad* of the time concerned to fill in the details.

Now the Islamic scheme of the state answers precisely to these demands. The *nass* ordinances of Qur'an and *Sunnah* outline to us the principles and fundamental features which a state must possess in order to be Islamic; for the rest, we are expected to exercise our *ijtihad* in accordance with our understanding of the two sources and the particular needs of our time. Such a scheme precludes, of course, an imitation of political concepts evolved in non-Islamic civilisations (without any regard to whether they agree or disagree with the teachings of Islam). Imitation is the opposite of creativeness—and the Prophet's ﷺ Message visualises a polity which would be creative in its own right under the inspiration of Islam. Those who blindly subscribe to non-Islamic political concepts on the plea that they are "modern" not only deny, by implication, Islam's claim to completeness in the *ideological* sense but also militate against the idea of Pakistan as such, for, if Islam is not to be the guiding principle of the state, why have a "Muslim" state at all?

But this is just what many of our intelligentsia seem unable to grasp. They do not realise that a state devised in the name and for the sake of a religious community must be, in the very nature of things, an *ideological* state; otherwise, the innermost purpose of our creating a state is defeated.

It appears to me, therefore, that the main problem now facing the members of Pakistan's Constituent Assembly is to avoid thinking in Western terms of state and nation and to think in Islamic terms instead. Apart from the obvious warning held out by the social and political picture of the West—internecine struggles and wars, social demoralisation, economic injustice (or, alternatively, abolition of all personal liberty)—there is another, no less weighty, reason for us to avoid imitating the political forms so characteristic of the Western world; and that reason is the opportunity, never before offered to a Muslim nation in modern history, to start with a clean slate and to establish an almost entirely new polity—a polity which would truly deserve the adjective "Islamic". If we neglect this momentous opportunity, if we shirk the responsibilities, difficulties, and perhaps even the dangers which so stupendous a reorientation of our life might bring with it, we will prove no more than that we are unworthy of the great possibility which God, in His infinite bounty, has now unfolded before us: the possibility of demonstrating, to ourselves as well as to the millions of wavering, defeatist Muslims in other parts of the globe that the law of Islam is not merely a subject for dry-as-dust books and theoretical discourses but a living, dynamic, expansive programme of social life; a programme sovereign in itself, entirely independent of momentary "constellations" and therefore practicable at all times and under all conditions; a way of life, in short, that would not only not hamper our society's development but would, on the contrary, make it the most progressive, the most self-reliant and the most vigorous of all existing societies.

Law Eternal and Law Temporal

But to fulfil these hopes of ours, our ideas about the law of Islam must be freed from all the limitations imposed on them by centuries of time-bound *fiqh*. In short, we must restore the concept of the *shari'ah* to that clearness and conciseness, to that purity and obviousness which it possessed at the time of its enunciation, for it is quite futile to speak of the "eternal" values of the *shari'ah* and, at the same time, to lump it together with the results of human, however scholarly, *ijtihad*—a mistake committed by many learned Muslims from the third century A.H. onwards.

Because of its extreme importance for our future development, this problem has been discussed at length at the very beginning of this publication. Without a proper grasp of the functions of Islamic law, there can be no revival of Islamic thought; and without such a revival of thought, there can be no question of our ever attaining a truly Islamic form of the state.

It has been often pointed out in these pages that the *shari'ah*, being a divine law, cannot possibly have been made dependent on deductions, inferences or subjective conclusions of any sort but must be contained, in its entirety, in the positive, clear-cut *nass* ordinances of the Qur'an and *Sunnah*. All those *nass* ordinances are so wisely formulated that they can be applied to every stage of social development; while, on the other hand, many of the subjective conclusions of the *fuqaha'* were no more than a reflection of a particular time and intellectual environment and cannot, therefore, lay a claim to eternal validity. A society that would consent—merely out of respect for the greatness of its past—to be ruled forever by the thought processes of men who lived a thousand years ago would thereby sign the warrant of its own doom, for when thought ceases to be creative, spiritual death sets in.

We must, therefore, give up the ridiculous notion that whatever the great scholars of our past have thought about the divine law is identical with that law itself. Only the incontrovertible, self-evident *nass* injunctions of the Qur'an and *Sunnah*—"do this", "don't do that", "such-and-such a thing is right", "such-and-such a thing is wrong"—only these injunctions constitute the eternal, unchangeable *shari'ah* of Islam. There are, comparatively, only few such injunctions in the two sources; and, therefore, the true *shari'ah* is very much smaller in volume than the pseudo-*shari'ah* evolved through *fiqh*. But because it is so small in volume, the shari'ah cannot —nor was it ever intended to—provide detailed legislation for every exigency in life and therefore the Law-Giver meant us human beings to provide for the necessary, additional legislation through an exercise of our *ijtihad*. Whatever *ijtihad* legislation we may evolve under the inspiration of the two sources (occasionally even with the help of the *ijtihad* of past generations) will add up to what is best described as Muslim law—a changeable law, liable to amendments and improvements by ourselves and by those who will come after us; and this process must continue as long as Muslim society exists. To repeat it once more, the *shari'ah* concerns itself exclusively with what the Law-Giver has ordained in unmistakable terms as an obligation (fard) or put out of bounds as unlawful (haram); while the far larger area of things and activities which the Law-Giver has left unspecified—neither enjoining nor forbidding them in *nass* terms—is to be regarded as allowed (mubah) from the religious point of view; and this is the legitimate sphere of Muslim law. The existence of an amendable Muslim law, subject to the authority of the irrevocable, unchangeable Islamic law (the *shari'ah*), is indispensable to a healthy, progressive communal life, and so, in the last resort, to a genuinely Islamic life, for there can be no Islamic life where thought is stifled and creativeness killed.

A little while ago I have stressed the fact that, for a believing Muslim, the *shari'ah* is the only valid, permanent criterion of good and evil in man's actions and behaviour. Anyone who studies its ordinances will confirm the finding that none of them ever conflicts with the real nature of man and the real requirements of society at any time—simply because the *shari'ah* legislated only with regard to those aspects of human life which are not necessarily subject to change. Now this special characteristic of the divine law—its applicability to all stages and conditions of human development— presupposes that its ordinances cover, in the first instance, general principles only (allowing thereby for the necessity of time-conditioned variations in detail), and, in the second instance, detailed legislation in matters which need not be affected by changes due to human progress. Thus, wherever detailed *shari'ah* legislation is provided for, it invariably relates to such aspects of our individual and social existence as are independent of all time-conditioned changes of environment. Wherever, on the other hand, time-conditioned changes are indispensable for human progress (for example, in matters of governmental procedure, industrial legislation, and so forth), the *shari'ah* does not stipulate any detailed laws; it either lays down general principles only or entirely refrains from any legal enactment. And this is where Muslim law (in the above-mentioned, temporal sense of the word) comes to its own.

In cases where no detailed *shari'ah* legislation is forthcoming and, on the other hand, the interests of the community do call for detailed legislation, we must, first of all, look into the *shari'ah* for a general principle of law. If such a general principle is available—for example, in the prohibition of riba—it falls within the scope of Muslim law to evolve detailed legislation on the basis of the principle, or principles, laid down in this respect in the *shari'ah*. Occasionally, we may be confronted with problems entirely untouched by the *shari'ah*—cases with regard to which neither detailed legislation nor a general principle is formulated in the *nass* of the two sources; and in such cases we are entirely free to formulate our own laws, taking only the spirit of Islam and the community's welfare into consideration.

Hence, Islamic law leaves a very large field of legislation open to temporal Muslim law, on the understanding that the latter's enactments shall not on any account contravene the spirit of Islam in general, or any *shari'ah* injunction, in particular. To be more precise, the legitimate field of Muslim law comprises legislation regarding (a) details in cases where the *shari'ah* provides a general principle but no detailed laws, and (b) principles and details in cases not covered by *shari'ah* laws at all.

On Constitutional Forms

On the basis of these reflections, we now begin to understand that many of the popular notions in respect of the forms and functions of an Islamic state are entirely erroneous. I am referring, in particular, to the idea prevalent among many pious Muslims that there could be only one form of state deserving the adjective "Islamic"—namely, the form manifested under the Four Rightly-Guided Caliphs—and that, therefore, any deviation from that model would detract from the Islamic character of the state. This view, we may safely assume, arises from a misconception of the problem; for, in reality, there is no "specific" form of the Islamic state owing to the fact that the *shari'ah* allows for a great latitude in governmental method and procedure.

The *shari'ah* lays down no more than a few cardinal principles to which any constitution must conform in order to be Islamic; beyond that, it leaves a vast field of constitution-making activity to what I define as a changing, time-conditioned Muslim law. Those cardinals, *shari'ah* points (which shall presently be discussed) were fully evident in the state of, say, 'Umar the Great: and therefore, his state was Islamic. But we must not forget that, in the unwritten constitution to which the Islamic Commonwealth conformed, in 'Umar's time, there were side by side with explicit *shari'ah* laws, many institutions and legislative enactments not derived from the *shari'ah* as such but from purely common-sense (*ijtihadi*) considerations directed at administrative efficiency, public welfare and so forth. In as much as all these enactments received the legal sanction of the government of the day, embodied in the person of the Caliph, they became the valid Muslim law of the time; and in as much as that particular Muslim law scrupulously refrained from contravening any *shari'ah* injunction, the state was Islamic in every sense of the word. But, as I have pointed out more than once, Muslim law can never be static; and this is particularly true with regard to the role which it must play in constitution-making. It is quite conceivable (I should rather say, unavoidable) that different times and a different intellectual and economic environments give rise to very different conclusions as to the best means of achieving administrative efficiency, social equity and public welfare—and so quite a big proportion of the constitutional enactments must vary accordingly. This cannot, of course, affect those elements of the constitution which are laid down by the *shari'ah* and are therefore unchangeable. But, leaving the *shari'ah* fundamentals apart, it is obvious that an Islamic Constitution to be evolved thirteen hundred years after the Rightly-Guided Caliphs may legitimately differ in more than one point from that which was valid in and for their time.

It is, however, not even necessary to postulate a time-distance of thirteen centuries in order to understand that the requirements of one time with regard to Muslim law—and, hence, to a good deal of the Constitution of the State—do considerably differ from the requirements in this respect of an earlier period. Even within the short span of a few decades, the Rightly-Guided Caliphs varied their administrative methods (or, as we would say today, the constitution of the state) in many a point. As an illustration, let us take the problem of electing the head of state. There was, naturally, no difference among the Companions as to the principle of elective government as such, for the *Shari'ah* law in this respect is clearly formulated in the Qur'an:

وَأَمْرُهُمْ شُورَىٰ بَيْنَهُمْ

"Their [i.e., the Believers] affairs are transacted by consultation among themselves" (Al-Shura 42: 38).

But though it is beyond doubt that the head of state must be elected—which is one of those cardinal points of Islamic law to which I have alluded above—the law does not specify the method of election; and so the Companions regarded the method of election, rightly, as something outside the scope of the *shari'ah*; as something that is, and could be, varied in accordance with the needs of the time and the best interests of the community. Thus, the first of the Rightly-Guided Khulafa, Abu Bakr, was elected by the chiefs of the Muhajirs and Ansaar present in Madinah at the time of the Holy Prophet's ﷺ demise. On his deathbed, Abu Bakr designated 'Umar as his successor, and this choice was subsequently ratified by the community (ratification being, in this case, equivalent to election). When 'Umar, in his turn, was dying, he entrusted an electoral body of six of the most prominent Companions with choosing his successor from among themselves; their choice fell on Uthman, who was thereupon recognised by the community as Umar's legitimate successor. After 'Uthman's death, 'Ali was proclaimed amir al-muminin by a congregation in the Prophet's ﷺ Mosque, and the community subsequently ratified this proclamation.

Hence, under each of these four reigns which we describe as "rightly-guided," the (unwritten) constitution of the state differed in a very important point: for nobody can deny that the method by which the head of state is elected is a constitutional point of great importance. The changing treatment of this point by the Companions shows that, in their opinion, the state constitution could be changed from time to time without making the polity any the less "Islamic" on this account. This opinion, needless to say, was absolutely correct. Islam demands of us no more and no less than that the constitution of the state should always faithfully reproduce the few fundamental, explicit rules laid down in this context by the *shari'ah*; while the rest of the constitution's contents may be left to communal *ijtihad* dictated by the needs of the particular time to which it applies—that is, to the Muslim law of the time.

Keeping these considerations in mind, we may now safely proceed with examining the *shari'ah* fundamentals of the Islamic state—or, to be more precise, those elements of legislation which must under all circumstances be embodied in the constitution of an Islamic state. For reasons shown in the preceding pages, I shall not approach this question from the historical angle. I shall not analyse the early forms of the Islamic state under the Four Rightly-Guided Caliphs, nor the forms into which the Muslim Empire subsequently developed; nor shall I refer to the conclusions arrived at in this context by the great fuqaha' or to the various political theories evolved later on by some of the most outstanding Muslim philosophers. Not that I underestimate the creative value of these *fiqhi* and philosophical works. Their authors' achievement was, from the intellectual point of view, often considerable, and not a few of them will forever retain places of honour in the history of Muslim culture. But this, exactly, is what we should remember: their place is in the history of Muslim culture and not in the practical politics of the present time. Our environment and our experiences are very much different from what those great thinkers of our past had experienced in their time—and so our political conclusions must differ in many vital respects from theirs, just as the conclusions of Muslims living five hundred years hence will necessarily, and materially, differ from ours. Nevertheless, so long as we truly desire Islam, much will be in common between our past and our present as well as between our present and our future; namely, the conviction that the *shari'ah* of Islam—expressed in the *nass* ordinances of Qur'an and *Sunnah*—is inviolable and cannot be changed; that it is the only permanent criterion of right and wrong in men's affairs; and that, therefore, it must forever remain the basis of any Islamic constitution as well as the starting point for all our constructive endeavours in the realm of Muslim law (or laws).

The First Principles

In an earlier part of our discussion, we have considered the purpose for which an Islamic state should be established and have found that this purpose consists in the achievement of Muslim unity and cooperation—a cooperation in terms of Islam and for the sake of Islam. Thus, the state is not an end in itself but only a means to an end, the end being man's surrender to the law of God. However well-intentioned he may be, man cannot attain to the fullness of Islamic life unless the society around him agrees to subject the dealings among all its members to the pattern visualised by Islam. Such an agreement as regard to action is not quite identical with agreement in beliefs. Belief is something that rests between man and God alone; but action and behaviour—especially social action and social behaviour—concern society as well. Hence the members of the society are responsible to each other for how they behave and what they do. This responsibility assumes a concrete aspect in the creation of a coordinating agency endowed with powers of command and prohibition; in a word, the state. In so far as the state derives its authority from the people's agreement on a particular scheme of social cooperation, it could be said that sovereignty rests with "the people"; but in so far as in an Islamic society, the people's agreement arises from their acceptance of the law of Islam, the Islamic state derives its sovereignty, in the last resort, from God.

To make the law of Islam the law of the land; to ensure the people's cooperation and to safeguard justice, and equity in terms of the Qur'an and *Sunnah*; to enable individual men and women to realise the tenets of Islam not only in their beliefs but also in the practical, socioeconomic concerns of their lives; to defend the community against disruption from within and attack from without; and to propagate Islam to the world at large; herein lies the innermost purpose and justification of the state as conceived in Mustafa's message. If it answers to these conditions, the State can be rightly described as "God's vicegerent on earth"—at least in that part of the earth which falls under its jurisdiction— for it holds power in trust from God.

Therefore; paragraph 1 of the Constitution of an Islamic State must say: "*The religion of the State is Islam; and the State derives its sovereignty from the Law of Islam.*"

The first and foremost duty of the state is to make the law of Islam the law of the land; in other words, to enforce the ordinances of the *shari'ah* in so far as they affect matters of social concern. We already know from our earlier investigations that the *shari'ah* is limited in extent, consisting solely of the *nass* ordinances of the two sources; and that, therefore, an additional, *ijtihadi* legislation is necessary to cover all the exigencies of communal life. But while we are, thus, at liberty to supplement the eternal Islamic law by temporal laws of our own, we are not at liberty to neglect any of the *shari'ah* rulings, be they detailed or general. The Qur'an is absolutely unequivocal on this point:

وَلْيَحْكُمْ اَهْلُ الْاِنْجِيْلِ بِمَآ اَنْزَلَ اللّٰهُ فِيْهِ ۗ وَمَنْ لَّمْ يَحْكُمْ بِمَآ اَنْزَلَ اللّٰهُ فَاُولٰۤىِٕكَ هُمُ الْفٰسِقُوْنَ

"Whoso does not judge by what God has sent down —these indeed are the evil-doers" {al-Ma'idah 5: 47).

Therefore, the constitution of the state must have a provision to the following effect: "All laws of the *shari'ah* bearing on matters of public concern form the inviolable, basic code of public law; and no temporal legislation, mandatory or permissive, shall be valid if it is found to contravene any stipulation of the *shari'ah*."

From the above, it becomes obvious that the state must make the necessary arrangements for a codification of the *shari'ah* bearing in mind its limitation to the *nass* of the Qur'an and *Sunnah*. A suggestion as to the lines on which such a codification should proceed has been made in the January number of *Arafat* (vol. I, No. 5, pp. 149-152), but I have no doubt that other scholars could suggest further improvements and amplifications regarding the method to be adopted. In order to remove a possible misapprehension in this respect, I should like to repeat what I have already said on earlier occasions. There is no question of "drafting" *shari'ah* laws, or of "deducing" them by any *fiqhi* process. No law can be regarded as a *shari'ah* law unless it is clearly laid down as such, in terms of command, prohibition or positive statement, in either of the two sources; that is to say, laid down in such a way that there can be no possibility of misunderstanding or interpreting it in various ways. This, indeed, is the definition of *nass*; and no passage of the Qur'an or of a *hadith* which does not conform to this definition can possibly have been intended by the Law-Giver to enunciate a law in the *shar'i* sense. If we keep this in mind, we at once realise that a codification of the *shari'ah* should not cause any special difficulties. Under the terms of reference to be issued to them, the scholars entrusted with this task will simply have to collect all *nass* ordinances forthcoming from the Qur'an and from authentic traditions and to leave aside all ordinances (or what some may regard as ordinances) which are liable to more than one interpretation; and the very small collection thus arrived at will represent an agreement, on a minimum basis, between all schools of Islamic thought. For, however much the 'ullama' may disagree about the meaning of such passages of the Qur'an and such *ahadith* as are liable to more than one interpretation, they are bound to agree as to the meaning of ordinances established as such in the *nass* of either of the two sources. Their task will be further simplified by the fact that, for the purposes of the state, only ordinances bearing on matters of social concern need be codified. This does not, of course, mean that the *shari'ah* as such is, or ever could be, restricted to matters of social concern only: it only means that the State, being a social organisation, is concerned with social matters only, and therefore requires of the *shari'ah* no more than a code relating to these matters. But this code it must have, otherwise it can never become an Islamic state.

And now, having decided the state's fundamental attitude towards the *shari'ah*, let us ascertain the method by which the state is to run and temporal legislation, whenever necessary, enacted.*

*(*Arafat*, vol.1, no.9, (July 1947).

Appendix VI

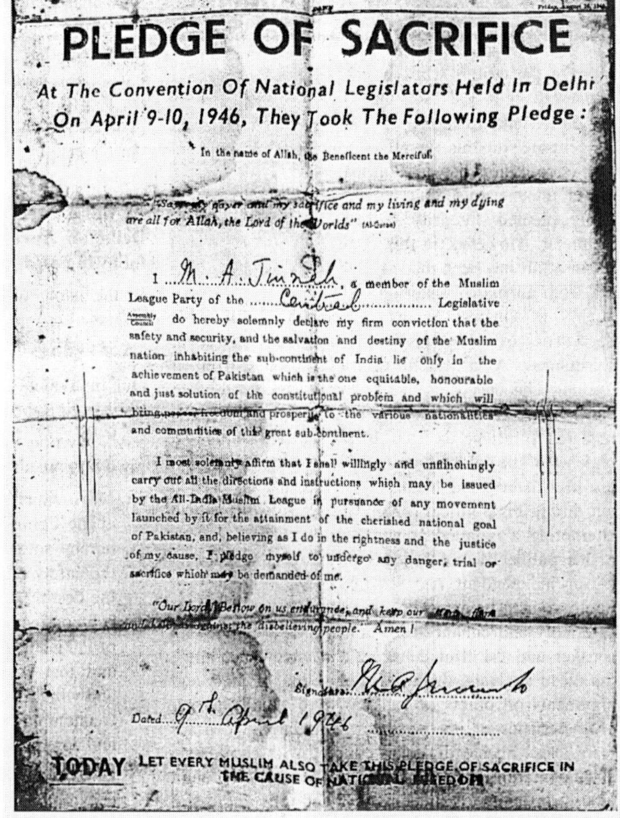

PLEDGE OF SACRIFICE

At The Convention Of National Legislators Held In Delhi On April 9-10, 1946, They Took The Following Pledge:

In the name of Allah, the Beneficent the Merciful.

"Say: [illegible] prayer and my sacrifice and my living and my dying are all for Allah, the Lord of the Worlds" (Al-Quran)

I ...M. A. Jinnah..., a member of the Muslim League Party of the ...Central... Legislative Assembly/Council do hereby solemnly declare my firm conviction that the safety and security, and the salvation and destiny of the Muslim nation inhabiting the sub-continent of India lie only in the achievement of Pakistan which is the one equitable, honourable and just solution of the constitutional problem and which will bring [illegible] freedom and prosperity to the various nationalities and communities of this great sub-continent.

I most solemnly affirm that I shall willingly and unflinchingly carry out all the directions and instructions which may be issued by the All-India Muslim League in pursuance of any movement launched by it for the attainment of the cherished national goal of Pakistan, and, believing as I do in the rightness and the justice of my cause, I pledge myself to undergo any danger, trial or sacrifice which may be demanded of me.

"Our Lord! Bestow on us endurance, and keep our [illegible] against the disbelieving people. Amen!

Signature: M A Jinnah

Dated: 9th April 1946

TODAY LET EVERY MUSLIM ALSO TAKE THIS PLEDGE OF SACRIFICE IN THE CAUSE OF NATIONAL FREEDOM

End Notes

1. Stanley Wolpert, *Jinnah of Pakistan*, Karachi, Oxford University Press, 1993, p-VII.

2. Concluding address, Muslim League annual session, Karachi, December 26 1943, Yusufi, ed. *Speeches, statements and Messages of the Quaid-i-Azam*, Lahore, Bazmi-Iqbal, 1996, volume III, p1821.

3. A non-substantial debate has been created by some liberals in the country on the sequence of these three unifying principles. During the rule of army dictator Musharf, a former federal minister Mr. Mahmud Ali, who belonged to, at one time East Pakistan, personally approached him and told him that he himself heard the Quaid putting Faith before Unity. On his evidence, the sequence at the hill side on the Islamabad Express Way was readjusted and Faith, Unity and Discipline as arranged in order of priority. As a man of legal understanding, the Quaid knew well that it is faith which unites and not unity which leads to faith.

4. Allama Iqbal, Presidential address, All India Muslim League session, Allahabad, 1930, in G. H. Zulfiqar, ed, *Pakistan As Visualized by Iqbal and Jinnah*, Lahore, Bazme-e-Iqbal n.d. p15-22.

5. Recorded Radio Broadcast talk to the people of the USA February 1948, in *Quaid-i-Azam Muhammad Ali Jinnah: Speeches and Statements 1947-1948*, Islamabad, Government of Pakistan, Ministry of Information, 1987, p157.

6. Abul A'la Mawdudi, *Islamic Law and Constitution*, tr.ed. Khurshid Ahmad, Lahore, Islamic Publication Limited, 1980, p218-219.

7. Muhammad Asad, *Principles of state and government in Islam*, Gibraltar, 1980, p21.

8. Muhammad Asad, *"What do we mean by Pakistan" in Muhammad Asad (Leopold Weies) Europe's gift to Islam* ed. M. Ikram Chughtai, Lahore, Sang-e-Meel Publication, 2006, vol-2, p910.

9. M. Ikram Chaghtai, 2006, p914.

10. Ibid, p914.

11. M. Ikram Chaghtai, 2006, p924.

12. Chaghtai, 2006, p922.

13. Ibid, p922-923.

14. Ibid, p923.

15. M.Rafiq Afzal, *Speeches, statements of Quaid-i- Millat Liaqt Ali Khan, 1941-1951*, Lahore, Research Society of Pakistan, University of the Punjab, 1987, p58.

16. Speech delivered at the Muslim University Union, Aligarh, March 6 1940, *Speeches, Statements and Messages of the Quaid-i-Azam*, ed. K.A.K. Yusufi, Lahore, Bazm-i-Iqbal, 1996, volume 2, p1159.

17. Dr. G.H. Zulfiqar, ed, *Pakistan, as Visualized by Iqbal & Jinnah*, Lahore, Bazmi-Iqbal.n.d. p32.

18. Address to Bar Association Karachi, January 25 1948, *Speech, Statements and Messages of the Quaid-i-Azam* e.d. K.A.K. Yusufi, Lahore, Bazm-i-Iqbal, 1996, Vol 4, p2669.

19. *Shari'ah* Academy, *Tasawur-i-Pakistan Baniyan-e-Pakistan Ki nazar main* (Concept of Pakistan as visualized by the Founders of Pakistan) Islamabad, International Islamic University, 2013. p82-83.

20. *Speeches and Statements of Quaid-i-Millat Liaquat Ali Khan 1941-51*, ed. M. Rafique Afzal, Research Society of Pakistan, University of Punjab, Lahore 1987, p229.

21. Ibid, p230.

22. Ibid, p230-231.

23. Ibid, p231.

24. Ibid, p232-233.

25. Ibid, p233-234.

26. Abul A'la Mawdudi, *Tehrik Azadi-i-Hind aur Musalman*, Lahore, Islamic Publication, 1999, Vol-1, p311-333.

27. Dr. Ishtiaq Hussain Qureshi, *'ullama in Politics* (1974), Karachi, Ma'arif Limited, 1974, 2nd Edition, p354.

28. Ibid, p351.

29. Ibid, p351-352.

30. Ibid, p352.

31. Address at the Hostel Parliament of Ismail Yusuf College, Jogeshwari, Bombay, February 1 1943. M. A. Harris ed. *Quaid-i-Azam*, 1976, Karachi, Times Press, p174.

32. The Qur'an, *al-Baqarah* 2:256.

33. The Qur'an *al-Kafirun* 109:6.

34. M.A. Harris, *Quaid-i-Azam*, Karachi, Times Press, 1976, p173.

35. The Qur'an, *al-Hajj* 22:41.

36. I.H. Qureshi, *The Struggle For Pakistan*, Karachi, University of Karachi, 1982, p312.

37. Malik Bennabi, *Islam in History and Society*, Kuala Lumpur, Berita Publishing, 1991. P52

38. Frantz Fanon, *The Wretched of the* Earth, New York, Cosmo Press, 1963.

39. Abul A'la Mawdudi, *Nashri Taqrirain* (Urdu), Lahore, Islamic Publication Limited, 1978.

40. For twenty-two unanimously agreed points of these *'ullama* see Annex I.

41. For names of *'ullama and mashaikh*. Please see Annex II.

42. Muhammad. Munir, *From Jinnah to Zia*, Lahore, Vanguard Books, 1980, p29.

43. Saleena Karim, *Secular Jinnah and Pakistan: What the Nation doesn't know*, Karachi, Paramount Publishing Enterprises, 2010.

44. Saleena Karim, 2010, p30.

45. Saleena Karim, 2010, p30.

46. K.A.K. Yusufi, ed. *Speeches, Statements and Messages of the Quaid-i-Azam*, Lahore Bazm-i-Iqbal, 1996, Vol-4, p 2563 (Interview with Doon Campbell, Correspondent, New Delhi, 21 May 1947).

47. Saleena Karim, 2010, p31.

48. Saleena Karim, *Secular Jinnah and Pakistan what the Nation Doesn't Know*. Karachi, Paramount Publishing Enterprise, 2010 P162-163. Saleena refers to the Hindustan Times, July 14 1947, where this interview was published.

49. Dr. Javid Iqbal, *Ideology of Pakistan*, Lahore Sang-e-Meel Publication, 2005, p16.

50. *Quaid-i-Azam Muhammad Ali Jinnah, Speeches and Statements 1947-1948*, Islamabad, Government of Pakistan Ministry of Information, 1989, p46-47.

51. M.A. Harris (1976) quoted above, p174.

52. Eid message to the Muslims of India, September 8 1945 in K. A. K. Yusufi, *Speeches, Statements and Messages of the Quai'd-i-Azam*, Lahore Bazm-i-Iqbal, 1996, Vol-3, p2053.

53. M.A. Harris, ed. Quaid-i-Azam, Karachi, Times Press, 1976, p173.

54. Al-Qur'an *Al-'Imran* 3:19.

55. Al-Qur'an *Al-Maidah* 5:3.

56. K.A.K. Yusufi, *Speeches, Statements and Messages of the Quaid-i-Azam*, Lahore Bazm-i-Iqbal, 1996, Vol-2, p1181.

57. K.A.K Yusufui, 1996, Vol-3, p2010.

58. K.A.K Yusufui, 1996, Vol-3, p1821.

59. Eid message to the Muslims of India, September 8 1945 in K.A.K. Yusufi,1996, Vol-3, p2053.

60. *Quaid-i-Azam Muhammad Ali Jinnah Speeches and Statements as Governor General of Pakistan*, Government of Pakistan, Ministry of Information, 1989, p155.

61. K.A.K. Yusufi, *Speeches and Messages of the Quaid-i-Azam*, Vol- III, p1766.

62. K.A.K. Yusufi, 1996, Vol-III, p1856-57.

63. Address to civil, naval, and military officers, Khaliq Dena Hall, Karachi, October 11 1947, in *Speeches and Messages of the Quaid-i-Azam,1947-48*, Islamabad, Govt of Pakistan, 1989, p74; also K.A.K Yusufi, Vol-IV, p2623-24.

64. Speech at Sibi Darbar, February 14 1948, *Quaid-i-Azam Muhammad Ali Jinnah Speeches and Statements as Governor General of a Pakistan*, Government of Pakistan, Ministry of Information, 1989, p142, Also K.A.K. Yusufi, 1996, Vol-IV, p2682.

65. K.A.K. Yusufi, op.cit, Vol IV, 1996, p2691.

66. K.A.K. Yusufi, op.cit,Vol IV, 1996, p2692.

67. *Quaid-i-Azam Muhammad Ali Jinnah Speeches and Statements 1947-48*, Government of Pakistan, 1989, p125.

68. *Quaid-i-Azam Muhammmad Ali Jinnah, Speeches, Statements and 1947-1948*, Govt of Pakistan, 1989, p94.

69. K.A.K Yusufi, Speeches and Statements, Vol-III, p2010.

70. *Quaid-i-Azam M. Ali Jinnah Speeches and Statements*, July 1 1948, 1947-48 Ministry of Information, Government of Pakistan, Islamabad, 1989, p271.

71. Sultan Zaheer Akhter, *Shayed Keh Tery Dil main uter jai meri baat*, Rawalpindi, Tanzim Karkunan-i-Pakistan, 1998, p23-24.

72. Address at All India Muslim League 1939 reported in Daily *Inqalab* Lahore, October 22, 1939. Quoted by Dr. Safdar Mehmood, "*Quaid wanted Islamic, democratic state*", Dawn Pakistan Day Supplement, March 23, 2002 p-V.

73. Agha Ashraf, *Muraqa Quaid-i-Azam*, Lahore, Maqbool Academy, 1992.

74. Annex-III.

75. Javid Iqbal, *Ideology Of Pakistan,* Lahore, Sang-e-Meel Publications, 2005, p12-14.

76. Ibid, p15.

77. Wilfred Cantwell Smith, *Islam in Modern History,* New York, Mentor Books, 1957, p217-219.

Glossary

Adl Justice, balanced, equity, fairness.

Ahl-i-hadith refers to religious movement that emerged in northern India in the mid-nineteenth century. They developed a more or less literalist approach toward the Qur'an and hadith.

Ahliyah Ability, eligibility, competence, skill, fitness.

***Al-Aziz* (The Mighty One)** The Strong, one of the Names of Allah. The Most Esteemed, The Exalted in Might.

'Alim: 'Alim or 'Alīm عليم is one of the Names of Allah, meaning "All-knowing One". It is also used for a learned man, scholar, knowledgeable person.

Allama Very wise or learned (honorific title bestowed on some learned person or erudite scholar).

Amanah Trust, honesty and loyalty.

Amir al-Muminin Commander of the Faithful, is a title designating the supreme leader of an Islamic community.

Amir Leader, commander, prince.

Baraelvi Any one graduated from a Baraelvi seminary located at Rai Baraeli in India. Also a follower of Maulana Raza Ahmad Baraelvi.

Deobandi A graduate of Deobandi seminary a known religious seminary, at Deoband in India.

Dewnagri The Sanskrit script used for writing in India.

Din Used in the Qur'an at around 85 places meaning - the way of life. The Qur'an calls Islam as din, it includes belief, devotions, social, economic, political and legal and cultural teaching of Islam.

Dini madaris Islamic seminaries.

Diyana Honesty, integrity, conscientiousness, fidelity, faithfulness.

Ehtisab Accountability, and responsibility.

Eid Festival, feast two major feasts of the Muslims are called Eid al Fitr and Eid al Adha.

Fiqh Fiqh is an Arabic term derived from the root word faqiha, meaning deep and comprehensive understanding of din. A Faqih is a scholar specializing in law and theology.

Ganpati puja A 10-day festival marking the birth of the elephant-headed deity Ganesha, the god of prosperity and wisdom. In Hindu tradition, Lord Ganesha is worshipped before any other deity or puja because he is considered the remover of obstacles.

Gau puja Gau Puja refers to the worship of the cow as Goddess Kamadhenu in Hinduism.

Hadith/ahadith Hadith, literally a report, a narration, technically authentic record of what the Prophet of Islam, said, did, or endorsed.

Hakim Hakīm, literally, wise one, a ruler.

Halal Lawful in Islamic law (fiqh).

Hanafi The school of thought followed by Imam Abu-Hanifah (699-767CE).

Hanbali Follower of Imam Ahmad bin Hanbal (780-855CE), one of the four Sunni schools of fiqh, known especially for its role in the codification of early theological doctrine, based on the interpretation of fiqh by Ahmad ibn Hanbal.

Ibadat Ibadah, also spelled ibada meaning worship, service or servitude.

Iman Faith, belief, or conviction.

Ijtihad Ijtihād, legal deduction based on the Qur'an and the Prophetic practice or sunnah

Ijma' Consensus of scholars.

Ijtima'yat Togetherness, communal unity.

Ittihad Concord, unity, alliance

Ja'fari Commonly followers of fiqh Ja'fari, established by Ja'far al-Sadiq, the 6th Shia Imam.

Jama'ah The community.

Jina Founding father of Jainism who claimed to attain liberation from karma.

Jumu'ah Friday also refers to the day of weekly congregation prayer of the Muslim.

Kafir-i-Azam **(great denier)** Mazhar Ali Azhar an Ihrari leader, used this word to insult the Founding Father M. Ali Jinnah.

Khalifah: **A Khalifa or (Arabic: خليفة; caliph)** it also means successor, ruler or leader.

Khilafah Caliphate, denotes the office of the political leader of a Muslim state.

Kufr Disbelief, unbelief, to be thankless, to be faithless, or ingratitude.

La ilaha illa-Allah There is no deity worthy of (worship or unconditional obedience) except Allah Subh'anahu Wa Ta-A'la.

Mazhab Any school of thought within Islamic jurisprudence.

Maghrib The west; the western quarter; the western countries; sunset.

Maliki One of the four schools of Islamic law, founded by Malik ibn Anas (711–795).

Ma'ruf Good, useful, known.

Mashaikh Plural of Shaikh. The word Shaikh also means spiritual leader or Murshid.

Masjid/masajid Place of worship for Muslims, mosque.

Maslak Used for schism, a sect.

Mas'uliyyah Accountability.

Maulavi It is a religious title given to graduates of religious schools.

Millat Community, nation.

Mufassir Exegete, scholar of Qur'anic studies.

Mujahid A person who engages in jihad, someone who struggles or fights against oppression, and injustice in order to establish justice, peace, and human rights.

Mulla Same as maulavi, title used for a religious scholar.

Mulukiyat Monarchy, it refers to a form of governance where a king or monarch holds power.

Munkar Wrong, immoral, vice.

Mushawart Mutual consultation, counsel, deliberation,

Nass A clear legal injunction divine decree, written law or canonical text.

Nawab Belonging to royal family, a prince.

Qadi A judge, expert in Islamic law.

Qibla The direction of the Ka'bah, in Makkah, toward which Muslims face to make their daily prayers.

Quaid In Urdu means Leader.

Qur'ani nizam-i- hukumat The system of government based on Qur'anic principles.

Quraysh The leading tribe with branches, who controlled management of Ka'bah and Hajj in Pre-Islamic period. The Prophet was born in the clan of Hashim tribe of Quraysh.

Ramadan It the ninth month of the Islamic lunar calendar, observed by Muslims worldwide as a whole month of fasting, prayer, reflection, and community welfare.

Rasool A prophet or messenger of Allah Almighty, to whom a shariah is given.

Riba In Arabic means to increase or to exceed and is commonly used for interest, declared prohibited by the Qur'an.

Salah Refers to Islamic prayer it is prescribed as an obligation on all Muslim male or female.

Salam Means peace. Islamic greeting Asslamu alaykum, means Peace be upon you.

Sardar A title of nobility that was originally used to denote, noblemen, chiefs, and other aristocrats. It also denotes a chief or leader of a tribe or group.

Shafi' One of the four Sunni schools of Islamic jurisprudence, founded by Muhammad ibn idrees al-Shafi (767–820 CE).

Shari'ah/Shara'ey Sharī'ah, meaning path to the watering place, technically it refers to the Divine injunctions in the Qur'an and the sunnah of the Prophet.

Shaytan Iblīs, One from Jinn, who is Known as Satan.

Shi'i The word Shi'i, or Shi'ite, literally means "one who is a partisan," or "supporter", of hazrat Ali. It is used for followers of Shi'i fiqh.

Shudh To become pure or purified, Hindu extremist movement to convent Muslims to Hinduism Known as karma shudhi.

Shura Consultation, or consultative decision making in Islam.

Sufiya Plural of sufi or a mystic.

Sultan Ruler, king.

Sunnah The tradition or way of the prophet Muhammad (Peace be upon him).

Ta'limat Teachings, instructions.

Tanzim Organization, cohesive body.

Tawhid The belief in Uniqueness and Oneness of Allah s.w.t. Tawhid is the core teaching of Islam.

Ukhuwah Brotherhood, based on faith and ideology.

'Ulama singular 'alim means scholar, learned person.

Ummah Community of the believers or Muslims.

Wilayat-e faqih Refers to the authority of the spiritual leader or Imam in shi'i political thought.

***Zakah:* Zakat (or Zakāh)** is one of the five pillars of Islam. It is a form of worship through contributing 2.5% of yearly savings to the poor and needy.

Index